# Taoist Lessons for Educational Leaders

*Gentle Pathways to Resolving Conflicts*

Daniel Heller

ROWMAN & LITTLEFIELD EDUCATION
A division of
ROWMAN & LITTLEFIELD PUBLISHERS, INC.
Lanham • New York • Toronto • Plymouth, UK

Published by Rowman & Littlefield Education
A division of Rowman & Littlefield Publishers, Inc.
A wholly owned subsidiary of The Rowman & Littlefield Publishing Group, Inc.
4501 Forbes Boulevard, Suite 200, Lanham, Maryland 20706
http://www.rowman.com

10 Thornbury Road, Plymouth PL6 7PP, United Kingdom

Copyright © 2012 by Daniel Heller

*All rights reserved.* No part of this book may be reproduced in any form or by any electronic or mechanical means, including information storage and retrieval systems, without written permission from the publisher, except by a reviewer who may quote passages in a review.

British Library Cataloguing in Publication Information Available

**Library of Congress Cataloging-in-Publication Data**

Heller, Daniel, 1953–
Taoist lessons for educational leaders / Daniel Heller.
p. cm.
Includes bibliographical references and index.
ISBN 978-1-61048-518-0 (cloth : alk. paper) — ISBN 978-1-61048-519-7 (pbk. : alk. paper) — ISBN 978-1-61048-520-3 (electronic)
1. School management and organization—Philosophy. 2. Educational leadership—Philosophy. 3. Taoism. I. Title.
LB2805.H385 2012
371.2001—dc23
2011049438

™ The paper used in this publication meets the minimum requirements of American National Standard for Information Sciences Permanence of Paper for Printed Library Materials, ANSI/NISO Z39.48-1992.

Printed in the United States of America

To Nina, my best friend

# Contents

Acknowledgments — vii

Introduction — ix

1. Balance — 1
2. Governance and Flexibility — 15
3. When to Act and When Not to Act — 29
4. Power Struggles and Conflicts — 41
5. Paradoxes of Leadership — 55
6. Themes and Images — 69

Conclusion — 79

References — 83

About the Author — 85

# Acknowledgments

I would like to thank Mary Greene, Wang JueFei, Ron Stahley, and Lien Yuan Hsiu for their willingness to be readers of my work. I would also like to acknowledge my family: Nina, Ben, Pam, Anthony, Namiah, and Socrates.

I would also like to thank SkyLight Paths Publishing for permission to quote from their publication *Tao Te Ching: Annotated & Explained*, copyright 2006. Translation, annotation, and introductory material by Derek Lin. SkyLight Paths Publishing, Woodstock, Vermont.

# Introduction

Imagine that you are the principal of the Goldwing Middle School, serving grades 6 through 8. You are pleased with this year's school opening. Teachers and students have settled into a productive and peaceful pattern. Parents appear satisfied, and the board has been quiet.

You are particularly pleased with the performance of Mr. Lind, the new Spanish teacher. He is both new to the profession and new to your school. You do not know him well yet, but you have high hopes. There is always that break-in period for a new teacher when problems can arise. So far, three weeks into the year, everything has been going well.

Then one Tuesday morning you find eighth grade student Jane Styles waiting for you outside your office. Naturally you invite her in and ask her what you can do for her. She tells you that she is having problems with a particular teacher, Mr. Lind.

Jane claims that Mr. Lind treats her unfairly by asking her to come up to the board to answer questions she does not understand. This embarrasses her. She also says that she doesn't like the way he looks at her. He makes her uncomfortable.

You consider your options. Is this a harassment issue? Jane's parents are influential people in the community. You had better proceed with caution. You could respond immediately, launching a formal investigation into the allegations. The first thing to do would be to interview Mr. Lind, and then call Mr. and Mrs. Styles to let them know what is going on. You would invite them in for a conversation with you. You would talk to other students, potential witnesses. And of course, you would interview Jane in more depth about the whole situation.

You could immediately go for the role of hero, either by taking the side of the beleaguered teacher or by taking the side of the powerless child. In either case, your bias would, at least in part, guide your actions. The key, regardless of anything else, is action. You cannot appear weak or hesitant where student feelings and safety are involved. Everyone involved will expect you to do something. You must control the situation and show that the school is on top of things.

There is, however, another way to respond to Jane. First, you could ask her clarifying questions until you were reasonably sure you understood her point of view. The next thing to do would be to do nothing. Take the time to think about what you have heard before doing anything. Reflect on the situation and the various paths it may take. Do not assume that anyone has exclusive rights to the truth. Knowing when and whether to act is crucial. Solve the problem with the least effort possible. Consider your various options.

Rather than interview Mr. Lind, you could have a conversation with him, informing him of Jane's perceptions and feelings. You might ask him if there is anything he does that might be misconstrued as looking at a student in such a way as to make her uncomfortable. You would also ask to hear his thoughts on why Jane feels embarrassed, what kind of student she is, and what her relationship with him is like.

Your mind remains open to all possibilities. You have made no accusations, drawn no conclusions. Your next step would be to inform Jane's parents that she is having difficulties with one of her teachers, and that you would like to meet with them, Jane, and the teacher to determine what, if anything, is going on. When you invite the parents to this meeting, you would also probe to find out what they have heard from Jane, and if they have already formed any opinion.

Before the meeting, you ask Mr. Lind to say as little as possible, and to let you direct the conversation. He agrees, especially since he is so new and does not quite understand what might be going on. He is feeling nervous and worried. Only you have spoken to all parties, thus having the broadest perspective. Everyone gathers for the conversation.

After introductions, you again ask Jane to describe her issues for everyone to hear. Both you and the parents ask clarifying questions. You try to allow the conversation to follow its natural path, again not taking sides, not making promises, not making any assumptions. On the other hand, you try to maintain an open, comfortable environment. You note the energies in the room, trying to work with them as opposed to trying to control them. The less you have to do, the better.

Working from you experience, you next ask Jane how she is doing in the class. You find out that she is not performing well. Jane admits that she rarely does her homework, a fact that Mr. Lind corroborates. He has sent one notice home about this situation. Mr. and Mrs. Styles did not understand how significant their daughter's homework issues were, and how her not doing it was hurting her progress in class.

You ask Mr. Lind how he uses the homework in class. He tells you that he asks students, at random, to go to the board and write answers to the various homework questions. Then you ask Jane if this embarrasses her. She says that it does because she does not have the answers, having not done the work. Her parents now show concern for her performance, placing responsibility on her for what is happening.

You ask Mr. Lind if he would be willing to give Jane some extra help after school, particularly on that evening's homework, and of course he agrees. Now that there is a cooperative and mutually supportive mood in the room, you ask about the second, potentially more contentious aspect of Jane's complaint.

You ask her to explain in more detail exactly what Mr. Lind does that makes her uncomfortable when he looks at her. She has trouble explaining what she meant by this, so you give her a way out. You ask if she thought, because she had not done her homework, that he was looking disapprovingly at her. She says "sort of."

Then you ask her if she feels guilty about the homework, which may be coloring the way she interprets his gaze. You further ask whether she does not like anyone looking at her when she does not know the answer. This too is met with a "sort of." Now you are ready to ask the big question: why are you really telling us that he is looking at you in a way that makes you uncomfortable?

Her answer is not surprising. She says that she is afraid that her parents, who are strict about school, will come down hard on her if she does poorly in Spanish class. She is very self-conscious when she is before the class without the answer.

She interpreted these feelings as being on the spot, which caused her to interpret his look as disapproving. Of course she felt uncomfortable when he interacted with her and she did not have the work or the answers. Her relationship with Mr. Lind was definitely uncomfortable. Now the whole problem is clear.

You, Mr. Lind, and the parents set up a communication system around Jane's performance in Spanish. Jane will get extra help after school. The parents will monitor the homework on their end. Mr. Lind will stay in contact with Mr. and Mrs. Styles. Jane now feels supported, and knows that she has not dug herself in so deeply that she cannot save the situation.

These two approaches to the problem reflect what this book is all about. The first scenario is all action. The principal sees the situation in terms of winners and losers, vindication and punishment. There are opposing sides around the problem, and the principal clearly has a plan of action, intending to bring the whole mess to a satisfying conclusion. We might call this reaction typical of Western thought: a thoughtful plan, immediate action, a good fight, winners and losers.

The second response is more contemplative, even gentler. The principal tries to stay neutral while gathering information before there is any overt action. He is not looking for winners and losers, but for a solution which can be satisfying to everyone involved. He wants to work with the situation, not control it. He wants to use the energies in the room to solve the problem, not to control these energies or put them into opposition to one another. We could consider this approach more Eastern, in particular reflecting Taoist ideas.

Chinese Taoism dates back many thousands of years. It is a belief system that describes the natural order of things, the natural unfolding of the universe and events. A central text in this tradition is the *Tao Te Ching*, or *Book of the Way*. Its author is unknown and is referred to as Lao Tzu, which means Old Master. This specific book dates back about 2,500 years.

Leaders can frame their actions through Taoist doctrines. All things have their way, and to know these ways allows one to work with them (Lin 2006, xix). The Tao helps us to understand emotional states and issues, thus allowing us to work productively with others (Lin 2006, xx). The Tao counsels reflection before action, going with the natural flow instead of trying to control it.

The Tao would have leaders be humble, They should be behind those they lead. They should not take glory in accomplishment or victories. They should be benevolent to their enemies as well as their friends. We are not to act rashly, or even at all unless it is necessary. To solve a problem with no action is the best. To plan and be prepared is the way.

Taoism insists that leaders act with virtue above all else. They need to remain as neutral as possible, doing what is right, not what their emotions tell them. Theirs is not to control a situation so much as to work with it. The principal should allow the situation to unfold as naturally as possible, limiting her action and need for control.

A second Taoist text, *The Art of War*, further emphasizes the application of these ideas to leadership and conflict. Although the author, Sun Tzu, was a great military strategist, his words from more than two thousand years ago can easily be applied to the leadership issues and conflicts encountered by a school principal.

The text is a thorough analysis of conflict, with the goal of resolving that conflict in one's favor without ever having to do battle (Cleary 1988, vii). As seen throughout the *Tao Te Ching,* battle should be avoided at all times. When it cannot be, battle is the last option, and even then should be no larger than necessary to accomplish the goal (Cleary 1988, xiii).

The Tao asks leaders to analyze situations fully, using the natural energies already present to resolve conflict with the least amount of effort or doing

(Cleary 1988, xiv). Sun Tzu wrote *The Art of War* during the period in Chinese history known as the Warring States, when war was a common occurrence. Thus, he was in a position to practice and apply his understanding of conflict resolution.

In the second example of Mr. Lind, the principal does not actually do much, nor is there any real fighting going on. He simply allows natural energies to express themselves in such a way as to bring a successful solution to the situation.

According to Sun Tzu, a successful leader will act dispassionately, acknowledging and understanding all of the forces and individuals involved in the conflict before taking any action. Like the Taoist sage, the leader does not take sides as much as act virtually, doing what is right in the given context. The leader acts with compassion, even for his enemies, an idea clearly expressed in the *Tao Te Ching*.

Leadership includes high moral and intellectual standards, even more so than courage and cleverness. Sun Tzu's words echo those of the *Tao Te Ching* in this regard. *The Art of War* also admonishes the victorious leader not to belittle or punish those defeated, but rather allow them to withdraw with their dignity intact.

Going back to the case of Mr. Lind, the principal did indeed find out as much information as possible before deciding how to proceed. She did not take sides, she did not try to hurt or defeat anyone, and she respected all parties. In effect, her strategies minimized any conflict and maximized communication in a safe environment. This is the Taoist goal, to avoid battle, amass information, remain as neutral as possible, and act virtuously.

This book does not offer Taoist ideas as a replacement for typical Western strategies. Instead, it offers an alternative to the usual response. It adds another strategy to the leader's bag of tricks. One way may not be any better than the other way, but depending on the situation, a wise leader might choose one over the other.

Throughout the book, passages from these two Taoist works are explained and applied to issues common in educational leadership. They could as well be applied to leadership activity in any field. The idea is to make the words of the Tao as concrete as possible, offering application, not just discussion.

The author offers numerous illustrations of Taoism in practice. Many of these situations come from his own experience. Of course, these examples are somewhat idealized to illustrate the point. In actual experience, the results of any of these situations might have not been so successful. One cannot account for all circumstances and possibilities in a model.

Each chapter addresses one major theme of the *Tao Te Ching* as it relates to educational leadership. Each chapter ends with two case studies. Each case study includes a number of discussion questions to help the reader reflect on the material and probe more deeply into the concepts the chapter has developed. Hopefully, these scenarios and questions will provide the opportunity for group conversation and problem solving practice.

Hopefully, by the end of the book the reader will have accumulated sufficient understanding of Taoist principles to begin applying them to situations in educational leadership on his or her own. The goal is not to become an expert on Taoism. Rather, it is to learn new approaches to leadership in general and in specific to educational leadership.

The text uses several different translations of these Taoist works. In this way, the reader can gain a sense of the richness of the text, as reflected in the various translations. Hopefully, the reader will go on to examine the *Tao Te Ching* and *The Art of War* directly for himself or herself.

The author is not a scholar of Chinese philosophy and culture. He has, however, read these works many times and has attempted to apply their lessons in his own professional and personal life. They have not always been successful, perhaps due to misunderstanding as much as anything else.

This book is offered to challenge the reader's thinking, the way the reader sees the world, and the way he or she acts in that world. Hopefully, the reader will learn some new ways to perform the tasks and meet the challenges of educational leadership.

*Chapter One*

# Balance

### THE MIDDLE ROAD

The Tao counsels us to balance our actions, to keep to the middle road. Extremes are dangerous, as are absolute points of view. Leadership is situational, even if one's underlying principles and beliefs are steady. When we may have to put out a fire, some occasions call for a garden hose whereas others call for fire trucks. Sometimes it is best not to react to a situation, but simply watch to see how events are developing. Chapter 9 of the *Tao Te Ching* tells us:

> Fill your bowl to the brim
> and it will spill.
> Keep sharpening your knife
> And it will be blunt. (Mitchell 1988, 9)

Overfilling a bowl simply wastes water, while stopping a bit short not only avoids the waste as described, but also avoids the waste of spilling the water as one carries the bowl. A principal can often find himself repeating his main point of philosophy in conversation after conversation with the same people.

Imagine how tiresome that must be for the listener. Beyond that, the constant repetition may actually turn the person away from the principal's ideas by making her hope never to hear them again. One has to find many ways of saying the same thing in order for it to be fresh and available to various listeners. One must also speak with actions as well as words. Leaders do not have to repeat their beliefs when their actions continuously reflect those beliefs. Repeating the same words over and over is out of balance.

## EXPECTATIONS

There is also the idea of expectations to consider. How much can a leader expect from someone at one time in terms of changed behavior? When a teacher comes to the principal at wit's end because of the behavior of a child, suggesting that more kindness and understanding might help may very well not be the appropriate recommendation at the time.

If anything, the teacher might respond by rebelling, seeing the principal as no help, and thus discrediting the leader and the advice. A better approach would be to ask the teacher what he or she has tried already, and then together brainstorm other possibilities, a little at a time. This is a balanced approach, looking at what has been done and then considering alternatives to try. What approaches would likely improve the situation, and which might make matters worse? In *The Art of War*, Sun Tzu speaks of intelligent action:

> Therefore the considerations of the intelligent always include both benefit and harm. As they consider benefit, their work can expand; as they consider harm, their troubles can be resolved. (Cleary 1988, 113)

If we try to pour too much into a stressed individual, our advice may be spilled on the floor or forgotten in the teacher's attempt to carry it back to the classroom. Think of a teacher who needed a great deal of guidance. Her approach was monotonous, low energy, and frankly boring. The principal could review teaching strategies with her, giving her many ideas to think about.

The results might be less than stellar. The leader would have done better to offer one suggestion, allow the teacher to try it, and then reflect upon its success or failure before moving on to another idea. In one's zeal to improve the situation, one can undoubtedly overwhelm the teacher.

## AVOIDING EXCESS

Have you ever felt like a blade that someone constantly pounded and sharpened? When a supervisor never lets up, the supervisee has no chance to reflect, to engage in his own thinking and problem solving, and eventually, as can happen, breaks under the pressure. Extreme approaches lead to extreme results. Too much of anything usually results in a disappointing situation. As the Bright-Fey translation says, when one acts with excessive behavior

> all that you get is a
> strained
> dulled split

>   and broken
>   deformation of the miraculous (Bright-Fey 2006, 62)

The trick is to allow enough time for events to work themselves out. Gentle guidance until someone is ready for deeper contemplation will move the situation without breaking the players. Out of respect for others, a good leader will always nurture before demanding, guide before pushing, and lead before dragging. As the leader increases the pressure on an individual to change, the possibilities for improvement will eventually become clear. Take a balanced approach.

Twice in my career, I have counseled teachers out of the profession. This was only after months of conversation, offering guidance, suggesting goals and strategies, and the like. One cannot go from zero to sixty instantaneously. This is not fair to either party. First, the leader tries to save the individual through a plan of improvement, and only after this has been exhausted is it time to move the person along to a more suitable career.

Even here we are not fully in control of the situation. There are times when a leader wishes to have more time to work with someone, only to find herself restricted by contractual time restraints. Another year of probation could have provided the room needed to help the teacher make the necessary adjustments.

Without that luxury of time, the principal has to assess the risk in keeping the teacher on, effectively granting tenure, on the hope that she can help bring him to a point where future growth is assured. To go back to the passage, would the leader have to pour too much water into the glass too fast, would she have to pound the sword too hard in a short period of time, to be successful?

## THE BALANCING ACT

In chapter 77 of the Tao, the writer tells us that

>   The Tao of Heaven
>   Reduces the excessive
>   And adds to the insufficient (Lin 2006, 155)

The Bright-Fey translation offers this rendering of the Chinese:

>   equalizing and balancing out and resolving
>   are the ways of heaven (359)

Everything is moderation. A good leader takes the time to understand the situation, reflect upon it, and then act deliberately and with dispassion. In other words, always keep an even keel. Too much running around and flapping of arms does no one any good. On the other hand, to fail to improve areas of weakness is inexcusable.

A school system once hosted the famous educational psychologist Madeline Hunter for three days of whole district inservice. She made a point of teachers checking for understanding while conducting lessons. Unfortunately, she gave one strategy which was so simple that in the hands of the staff it became excessive and ultimately nonproductive.

She suggested that teachers ask students whether they were understanding the lesson by having them put a thumb up for yes, down for no, and sideways for not sure. This should give the teacher valuable information while preserving the anonymity of each student.

This technique was too easy to be true, and everyone was ready to apply it the first day classes resumed. You can guess the outcome. Particularly in high school, where a student might have as many as six classes in a day, teachers used this checking device all day long, until it became a joke, and the inevitable single digit salute began to replace the upward thumb.

Too much of a good thing . . . too much lecture, too much discussion, too many rules; whatever becomes excessive begins to lose its meaning.

So often in public schools we dedicate each year to some specific new strategy or theme. We devote all of our energies to this one idea, and other good ideas fall by the wayside. Eventually, this new idea will be overplayed and fall by the wayside as well.

This breeds cynicism among teachers and administrators alike. If standards are a good thing, then we will have hundreds of them. If students are behaving poorly, then we will write dozens of rules. If we decide that we want to recognize student achievements, all of a sudden we are giving out dozens of awards each week, until the awards no longer hold much meaning.

The opposite is true as well. A principal may have to deal with a poor teacher whose incompetence has been tolerated for years because he was really in the system to be an athletic coach. He did, perhaps, bring in many championships. However, he also treated students poorly in his classes, scarcely knew his subject, and violated some basic legal procedures due to his ignorance of what was going on around him. Too little had been done concerning the behavior of this individual.

A school leader actually did reprimand this teacher, and even the union did not contest the situation, since the violation was an obvious legal matter. However, when she ventured into the territory of inappropriate language in front of students, the union offered such remarks as, "X bleeds the school colors." This was an example of "the insufficient" which had to be confronted. The rule of thumb, even stated by the teacher's immediate supervisor, was to leave the situation alone.

## LEARNING TO PICK ONE'S BATTLES

A good leader picks his or her battles. To fail to respond to subpar performance, or performance harmful to students or others in the institution, is to fail to add to the insufficient. There is no reason to "go after" people, but there is a reason to help everyone understand the importance of what each teacher is doing, and then to create an atmosphere and system which supports people's best efforts, again providing supports for those who need them until improvement occurs or the need for the individual to move on becomes clear.

Another example of the excessive is overreaction. Think of a school of 1,500 students. In theory, that would mean approximately 3,000 parents. Yet, that school could be turned on its ear by complaints from two or three sets of parents. If one were to consider the fact that there were another 2,994 parents who were not concerned, then such issues would not reach the board level and somehow enter into major policy discussions.

To lose moderation is to lose everything. No wind and the sailboat does not go anywhere. A gale and the boat may founder. The wise leader will try to keep the operation level, finding and keeping a natural rhythm that is comfortable but also just tense enough to keep everyone alert and on his or her toes.

## FLOW WITH THE RHYTHMS OF THE SITUATION

We might consider that optimal natural rhythm part of the Tao of the school, the way it is meant to run. It indicates a condition of comfortable alertness and seriousness of purpose with a sense of humor. Don't get excited; just get things done.

The twenty-eighth chapter of the Tao is crucial to understanding this concept of calm, even-tempered leadership.

> Know the masculine, hold to the feminine:
> Be the watercourse of the world.
> Being the watercourse of the world,
> The eternal virtue does not depart
> Return to the state of the infant.
>
> Know the white, hold to the black:

> Be the standard of the world.
> Being the standard of the world,
> The eternal virtue does not deviate
> Return to the state of the boundless.
>
> Know the honor, hold to the humility:
> Be the valley of the world.
> The eternal virtue shall be sufficient,
> Return to the state of plain wood.
>
> Plain wood splits, then becomes tools.
> The sages utilize them,
> And then become leaders:
> Thus the greater whole is undivided. (Lin 2006, 57)

In this chapter, the writer considers potentiality. By reserving action until a situation is well known, the leader maintains many possibilities for action before committing to one. There exists a vast array of characteristics, stances, and states of mind a leader may take in any given situation. At all times, the leader should act with humility ("Know the honor, hold to the humility").

For instance, the first line of the verse above reminds us to use both masculine (active) and feminine (contemplative) aspects of ourselves. Again, we can see the balance here of the excessive (all action) and the overpassive (all reflection). How many times did you or someone you knew act too quickly only to discover that the situation was not what he or she thought it was? How many times have you seen a good idea destroyed by discussing it until it was no longer recognizable as anything?

There is an incident in the hallway, and we are all action, quadrupling supervision between classes, while being insufficiently reflective, not bothering to think through the causes of the incident. Someone suggests that we allow students to use the bathrooms without passes, and we go into reflective mode, listing every possible reason why this is a terrible idea, instead of being more active and perhaps piloting a program for a week or two in order to see what actually happens. No action and too much action are equally ineffective.

The best course of action is to become like an infant, innocent, intuitive, and in tune with the world. An infant has not had time to cover over its natural oneness with the universe, and thus acts spontaneously as required by the environment, by circumstances as they are. It is neither right nor wrong. It simply does what needs to be done without need for praise or blame.

As the "watercourse of the world," the principal stands in the middle of everything. He is the hub of the school, through which all events, in one way or another, flow. At all times, however, he or she must hold on to virtue, to a knowledge of right and wrong, an understanding of ethical and unethical, a comprehension of fair and unfair. In this way, the principal stands as a vital filter for the activities of the school and thus gives direction to what occurs.

Once, a principal argued with a fellow administrator about the standards of conduct for athletes. Students who played sports were subject to stricter regulations concerning behaviors involving substance abuse than were students who belonged to other clubs or school organizations.

In the principal's opinion, this situation either treated athletes unfairly or implied that nonathletes were not also representatives of the school and thus worthy of such close scrutiny. Perhaps the rules even implied that athletes were the type of people who were more likely to abuse substances.

In any case, all substance abuse incidents eventually flowed through the principal, and his or her actions communicated more than the consequences, both school and legal, of the violations.

## A PATTERN FOR THE WORLD

The principal is always in the spotlight and, like King Solomon, he or she must demonstrate an even hand, a considered and balanced approach to leading the institution. Then that mind-set must become part of the institution's culture, shared by all members of the group. Balance starts with the person in charge, who must lead by example.

As the passage suggests, the balanced leader will know both black and white. Most important, though, the leader will serve as "the standard of the world." As such, he or she must demonstrate through action no deviation from virtue. All look to the principal to set the example, to walk the walk. As the Mitchell translation says:

> If you are a pattern for the world,
> the Tao will be strong inside you
> and there will be nothing you can't do. (Mitchell 1988, 28)

At the same time, a leader needs to retain humility. "Know the honor, hold to the humility / Be the valley of the world." No one likes a braggart. Besides, all victories are merely temporary, since another problem is sure to come along shortly after the first has been solved.

Many leaders have been guilty of this, seeking praise and recognition for what they felt was a job well done. Of course, they not only made themselves look weak and needy, but also they were inevitably hurt when some folk did not agree with what they had done.

Their disagreement leads the principal to judge the dissenters rather than consider their point of view. Again, what is lacking is a balanced point of view, a dispassionate approach to doing what is the best for everyone.

To follow the Tao is to follow that natural flow, to do what is right, not what one necessarily wants to do, or is told to do, or is the popular thing to do. One aligns with the Tao when one aligns with right action, with virtue, acting in a nonemotional manner.

By remaining "plain wood," the leader keeps all options open. Once the wood is split and made into a tool, it can be only that tool. By remaining uncarved, a leader can carefully choose action and method by waiting until he or she understands the situation. The Mitchell translation describes this phenomenon thus:

> The Master knows the utensils,
> yet keeps to the block:
> thus she can use all things. (28)

The "greater world remains undivided" because the leader acts in a manner which is with the flow, in tune with what the situation calls for, rather than in a haphazard and destructive way.

For instance, imagine having to work with a student who always cut his last-period study hall. Each cut resulted in an office detention, which the student also refused to attend. The missed detentions resulted in more detentions, which would eventually lead to suspension.

In this case, policy did not make much sense. Following it would merely inevitably lead to a power struggle which no one would win. Looking at the situation, what became clear was that the student found the study hall of no value, and would prefer to spend his time doing something worthwhile.

Sometimes a leader gets lucky. In this case, the principal was able to find the student something useful to do during that study hall time so that he would stay in school, avoid the whole cycle of cutting study hall and punishment, and do something useful instead. He spent the last forty-five minutes of his day recording books for learning disabled students. This solution had the added bonus of fulfilling the community service requirement for graduation.

## UNLIMITED POTENTIAL

We are all uncarved blocks of wood. We are potentialities waiting to happen. The Mitchell translation tells us that "The world is formed from the void, / like utensils from a block of wood" (28). If we allow ourselves to "form" too quickly or too slowly, not matching our responses to the natural flow of events quietly and with humility, we certainly run the risk of making a bigger mess than we started with. We need to wait carefully for the right moment to commit, to act.

Sun Tzu also makes reference to the leader's need to be flexible, ready to adapt to the requirements of each situation:

> So a military force has no constant formation, water has no constant shape: the ability to gain victory by changing and adapting according to the opponent is called genius. (Cleary 1988, 94)

We must lead dispassionately, but not without caring. We must lead not out of a need to be looked upon as wonderful, but out of a need to do, and a knowledge of, what is right. The good leader disrupts the flow of events as little as possible, and empowers others to do the right thing.

In chapter 29 of the *Tao Te Ching*, the writer once more confirms what we have been discussing. Lao Tzu tells us that leaders do away with extremes, including excess and arrogance (Lin, 59).

Leading is not unlike walking a tightwire—not too fast, not too slow. Be careful to avoid leaning too far to one side or the other. And finally, don't get cocky or overconfident. As soon as you think you know it all, that is the moment when someone or something or some situation will blindside you. The Mitchell translation reminds us of the dangers of trying to control a situation as opposed to working with it:

> The Master sees things as they are,
> without trying to control them.
> She lets them go their own way,
> and resides at the center of the circle. (29)

## BEING VS. DOING

In essence, the leader *is* the situation. One should be so mindful as to be acting automatically, like the infant, simply being in the process, allowing virtue to direct one's actions. This is a truly difficult concept, but my best attempt at explaining it is to say that one actually melts into the flow of events, becoming part of what is happening rather than apart from it trying to control it. The Dale translation ends chapter 29 as follows:

> The world's pulse is our pulse.
> The world's rhythms are our rhythms.
> To treat our planet with care, moderation and love
> is to be in synchrony with ourselves
> And to live in the Great Integrity. (Dale 2002, 59)

Taoism does not so much tell a principal what to do as it tells her how to be. If one can be in the moment, be virtue itself, somehow extinguish the duality that defines the distance between oneself and the event, then one will flow naturally into right action.

Consider an analogy with a baseball shortstop. The batter hits a screaming ground ball between second and third base. In one motion, the shortstop moves in the right direction, dives for the ball, catches it, rolls over, comes up throwing, and directs the ball directly into the glove of the player on first base. The batter is out. Can one say that the shortstop planned what he did, that he thought it through? I don't think so.

The player, for those few seconds, ceased to exist apart from the game itself. He was the game. The game was the player. This might be called the Tao of baseball, becoming one with the game.

In the same way, great leaders become so completely involved with their work that they are their work, and operate from the intuitive perspective of the infant, simply doing what should be done as part of the universal whole. Everything is in balance. The psychologist Mihaly Csikszentmihalyi calls this the flow state.

In this state of being, the self actually gets lost in the flow of events. With no self, there is no bias. The leader then does not act out of a need to be a hero, to please others, to be right, to gain revenge, to avoid conflict, or any other personal character inclination. On any number of occasions a leader may not do the right thing because he lets his personality interfere with taking the right action. At times, he may have taken the right action, but for the wrong reason.

In *The Art of War*, Sun Tzu writes:

> So it is said that if you know others and know yourself, you will not be imperiled in a hundred battles; if you do not know others but know yourself, you win one and lose one; if you do not know others and do not know yourself, you will be imperiled in every single battle. (Cleary 1988, 53)

Knowing oneself is vital. Only then can one be sure that actions are not based on personal bias.

## ACTING FOR THE RIGHT REASONS

Frequently a principal has experienced difficulty giving negative criticism to someone. There are probably all sorts of psychological reasons why this is difficult for her, but that is not the point. By having a need to be liked, she can fail to take care of personnel matters quickly enough to avoid problems.

Part of being a leader is telling people "no," or that what they are doing is not good enough. This does not make one popular, and that can be a weakness in a leader's approach to issues. The principal needs to recognize this in herself.

There are times when a principal makes a decision because he knows that his actions will make him a hero in the eyes of someone. Real heroes do not choose to be such, to run into burning buildings. Heroism just happens. However, if some leaders see an opportunity to bend a rule and thus make someone grateful to them and appreciative of them, they will do it.

Even if what they did turns out to be the right thing, the leader may too often be doing it for the wrong reason. Such reasons are no guarantee of an action being productive, virtuous, or appropriate. If the person involved was someone he did not like, he might just as easily not have bent the rule.

There are occasions when a principal chooses to enforce rules in order to dominate someone or to exact a kind of vengeance on a person who had made the leader's life difficult. Once again, this has led to legitimate action, but not for the right reason. If the principal could have immersed herself completely in the moment, like the baseball shortstop, then she would no longer have been acting from a sense of self, but rather from her being in the flow of the action.

I realize that this is beginning to sound otherworldly, but I am describing an ideal here. The point is to know oneself sufficiently, and to invest oneself in the situation so completely that one minimizes the possibility of action being tainted by personality and maximize one's being part of the natural flow of correct performance.

An action taken cannot be easily undone. Sun Tzu reminds us:

> A government should not mobilize an army out of anger, military leaders should not provoke war out of wrath. Act when it is beneficial, desist if it is not. Anger can revert to joy, wrath can revert to delight, but a nation destroyed cannot be restored to life. (Cleary 1988, 163)

Thus, part of balance is knowing when to act and when to wait patiently. Chapter 5 of the Tao states that

> Too many words hasten failure
> Cannot compare to keeping quiet. (Lin 2006, 11)

Many rules, too much talking, making decisions too quickly—these are not productive. What is productive is being quiet. While refraining from discussion or debate, one can simply observe. Taking the time for observation will allow the principal to better understand a situation and the need for action. On many occasions, a situation will resolve itself, while interference might make matters worse.

The Dale translation puts it this way:

> Countless words
> count less
> than the silent balance
> between yin and yang. (11)

The Mitchell version simply says, "Hold on to the center" (5). These terms "balance" and "center" come back again and again. The effective leader will always seek balance in whatever he or she does. In this case, the balance is between jumping into a discussion about something which appears problematic, or simply holding back to give events a chance to unfold.

## SOME EXAMPLES

A supervisor once worked with a teacher who came to talk with her frequently. He always had an issue to discuss, something which was making him unhappy. The supervisor would listen carefully and then respond. He would add more. The leader would again respond, and once more the teacher would continue the conversation. The exchange would become lengthy.

Finally, the supervisor realized that the teacher did not want to hear her suggestions or interpretations. He simply wanted to express his anxiety, to relieve the pressure he was feeling by talking. Realizing this, the leader changed her tactic. She still listened intently, but she did not offer a response.

The teacher simply wanted to be heard, and once he was, he left the office. The supervisor had been trying to fix a situation which did not need fixing. She needed to see what was happening before jumping directly into action.

Another teacher used to send long memos to the principal, who then thought it was his responsibility to show respect by writing back. However, if he wrote back, he would inevitably receive another long missive. The teacher always had to have the final word. Finally, the principal realized that if he did not write back, she would not continue the endless memo exchange.

Sun Tzu also has advice in this area:

> Skillful warriors are able to allow the force of momentum to seize victory for them without exerting their strength. (Cleary 1988, 67)

Clearly, the successful leader learns to determine when to apply effort in taking action, and when to let the flow of events reach the desired end by themselves. Why engage in battle when the enemy is already falling apart? Why try to impose an idea when the group is already moving naturally in the desired direction?

The themes of Taoism exist as an integrated and interwoven system of thought and being. For instance, the discussion of balance has already suggested and incorporated several other major themes: governance, selflessness and humility, paradoxes of leadership, when and when not to engage in conflict, when and when not to act, and flexibility. These concepts will become the subjects of subsequent chapters in this book. Any one concept necessarily works in concert with other concepts.

## CASE STUDY 1

*Lately there has been much conversation about student comportment, particularly around whether kids should be allowed to wear hats in the school. The custom among adolescents in the community is to wear hats, most often baseball caps. It is part of the "youth uniform."*

*There is one faction of teachers which absolutely believes that hats inside are inappropriate and rude. Many of the younger teachers see no harm in students wearing hats in the classroom. Of course, there are a number of teachers who really do not have strong feelings one way or the other.*

*Parents are also divided on the issue. The school board has been looking for a quick win on student behavior to demonstrate control for the parents' satisfaction. They see a hat rule as just such a victory. Make a rule and enforce it.*

*You bring the issue before the full faculty. The usual debate ensues, with teachers all over the map on the issue, strong in their individual beliefs. Some want a hard and fast rule, while others remind you of the debacle of the "formal shoe rule." Just trying to define a formal shoe, as opposed to a recreational shoe, was a monumental issue.*

*Attempts to administer the shoe rule resulted in inconsistencies, anger, and cynicism. You don't want to go through that again.*

*What you thought would be a ten-minute discussion has become an hour-long debate, with no end in sight. You could arrange to have the discussion continue at another time. You could impose a unilateral decision. You could establish a committee of teachers to study the situation. You know that the board has an interest in this issue, and that they are watching. What are you going to do?*

1. Which issues of balance can you see in this case? What lessons about balance discussed above can you apply to the situation?
2. Is there a middle road?
3. Is there another way to conduct the discussion?
4. Who should be involved in the decision?

5. What are the natural energy flows in the situation?
6. Can you impose a solution successfully?
7. What should you do first?

## CASE STUDY 2

*Two teachers are having difficulty working together. Teacher A generally supports you and the school. Teacher B does not respect you or the school. The two share a classroom, but they cannot amicably divide the space. They have both come to you with their individual complaints.*

*Teacher A likes to put seasonal displays on the bulletin boards. Teacher B generally does not use the boards, but won't allow her roommate to use more than exactly one-half the space. The same is happening with bookshelves, desk space, open or shut windows. You name it; they argue about it.*

*Their ill will is now affecting students, whom both teachers try to recruit to their side. You are worried that the teachers' unprofessional behavior may result in some actual altercations between students. Nothing blatant has happened yet, but you can feel that something is going to happen. You would like to avoid it, so you reinforce the rules around fighting so that you are sure all the students understand them and the consequences for breaking them.*

*You have spoken to each of the two teachers separately, but that has been of minimal help. Because of scheduling and classroom use constraints, you will not be able to separate these two teachers until the second semester, leaving you with about four months to worry about. Teacher A and Teacher B have now stopped talking to one another.*

*Teacher A has agreed to try to back off the conflict. He claims that it is not his fault anyway. He says that Teacher B will not compromise, is rude, and generally shows a belligerent attitude. She has longer tenure at the school and therefore insists that she be given preferential treatment. Teacher A believes that they both should be treated as professionals, priority treatment given to neither.*

*Teacher B has come to your office in a huff several times. She is threatening to go to the superintendent for a resolution to the situation, or even file a grievance against you with the union, claiming that you are treating her unfairly. You have assured her that both teachers are receiving the same treatment, sympathy, and assistance.*

1. Evaluate what you have already done with respect to balance.
2. Are there any lessons in this chapter which you could apply to this situation?

3. Is there a right and a wrong in this case?
4. What are the major issues and obstacles in this case?
5. Plan a course of action which is balanced. Justify your decisions and actions.
6. Should you involve others, such as your vice principal or the superintendent?

*Chapter Two*

# Governance and Flexibility

TAKING CARE OF THE PEOPLE'S NEEDS

A principal is responsible for the governance of a complex institution, not an easy task in the best of times. She has to deal with parents, taxpayers, teachers, students, other administrators, and government. Chapter 3 of the *Tao Te Ching* has this advice:

> The Master leads
> by emptying people's minds
> and filling their cores,
> by weakening their ambition
> and toughening their resolve. (Mitchell 1988, 3)

The wise ruler, then, cleans out the people's hearts of destructive desires while meeting their basic needs. The leader wants the people to be healthy and strong, but not seeking individual glory at the expense of others. The Dale translation puts the verse this way:

> The natural person
> Desires without craving
> And acts without excess. (Dale 2002, 7)

Sun Tzu is well aware of having to tend to the needs of staff. "Treat the soldiers well, take care of them" (Cleary 1988, 29). As we know, when conditions do not fulfill people's basic needs, everything else falls by the wayside. The principal is responsible for making sure that staff members have what they need, including peace of mind, security, a sense of worth. She foments a collaborative atmosphere and governance style.

## CREATING COMMON GOALS—VISION

Basically, the principal wants a situation in which all the staff members are working together in a comfortable, productive atmosphere. Individuals do not work against one another as in a zero-sum game.

Rather, they work together to attain common goals. In education, this is called having a vision and a mission which everyone in the school accepts. Such a vision is the result of the principal's working with the school and community to find some common definitions and goals.

Thus, Sun Tzu recognizes that a crucial task of leadership is to create a situation in which everyone in the organization shares the same goal, and that goal is also shared by the leader.

> The Way means inducing the people to have the same aim as the leadership, so they will share death and share life, without fear of danger. (Cleary 1988, 4)

Later in *The Art of War* he writes:

> Therefore those skilled in military operations achieve cooperation in a group so that directing the group is like directing a single individual with no other choice. (Cleary 1988, 150–51)

The vision, mission, and goals are so clear and mutual that actions are naturally attuned to the target, the good of the institution, and the welfare of the people. Building a common vision is critical for successful governance.

## REDUCING INTERNAL CONFLICT

In chapter 3, Lao Tzu explains that a good leader does not exalt some above others because this will lead to inner conflict among the people (Lin 2006, 7).

The Mitchell translation puts the point like this:

> If you overesteem great men,
> people become powerless.
> If you overvalue possessions,
> people will begin to steal. (Mitchell 1988, 3)

Once again there is a sense of balance here. By not offering excessive praise or reward, the leader governs fairly and without creating competition or resentment among the people. By not stressing the value of possessions, people are less likely to grasp for them.

How often have you confronted many needs with a limited budget? Only a few people can have new computers this year. Are the recipients "winners" and those who have to wait "losers"? This can cause stress and strife, unless the principal has a thoughtful reason why things are distributed as they are.

The good leader also must apply the idea of favors and disgrace to herself. She must not see self as the ultimate reality, but that which she serves.

Lao Tzu tells us that the great leader disregards the desire for favor and grace, and does not allow the fear of failure to rule his actions. A leader's responsibilities are not to worry about his standing, to protect his reputation. The responsibility is to act with virtue, doing the right thing, being stable and steady. He virtually ignores the self, fading into the background.

> Accolades can usher in
> great trouble for your body.
> censure can herald misery.
> Why can favor and disfavor
> both be harmful?
> Because both accolades and censure,
> when filtered through self as ego,
> always place us in jeopardy.
> But when the universe becomes your self,
> when you love the world as yourself,
> all reality becomes your haven,
> reinventing you as your own heaven. (Dale 2002, 27)

The Mitchell translation makes the point this way:

> What does it mean that success is as dangerous as failure?
> Whether you go up the ladder or down it,
> your position is shaky.
> When you stand with your two feet on the ground,
> you will always keep your balance. (Mitchell 1988, 13)

The thoughtful leader deals with needs more than desires. Where is the need for the new computers most urgent? Again, the leader would be wise to have a clear rationale for distributing limited resources in one way as opposed to another. The challenge is to govern with the natural flow of the situation. Where should the computers go naturally?

> Stop trying to control.
> Let go of fixed plans and concepts,
> And the world will govern itself. (Mitchell 1988, 57)

Lao Tzu is not recommending a laissez-faire approach. He is suggesting that good leadership involves doing what needs to be done as opposed to acting in accordance with a preconceived plan or for purely personal reasons. Governance must remain fluid to allow for constant adjustment as the situation shifts. Values are constant, but actions are situational.

# Chapter 2
# CONSISTENCY AND THE MIDDLE WAY

Even though the principal may act differently in different situations, the basis for these actions must be consistent beliefs and values. If a leader does not follow through on directives consistently, credibility will suffer. As Sun Tzu states:

> When directives are consistently carried out to edify the populace, the populace accepts. When directives are not consistently carried out to edify the populace, the populace does not accept. When directives are consistently carried out, there is mutual satisfaction between the leadership and the group. (Cleary 1988, 131)

The Tao points out a paradox of leadership which goes directly to the heart of governance:

> When there are many restrictions in the world
> The people become more impoverished
> When people have many sharp weapons
> The country becomes more chaotic
> When people have many clever tricks
> More strange things occur
> The more laws are posted
> The more robbers and thieves there are. (Lin 2006, 115)

Creating lots of rules and regulations does not create an orderly society. In fact, writing rules is often a simplistic way to deal with a problem. Rules point out what behaviors are and are not acceptable, but they do not get at the cause of the behaviors. They simply declare more behaviors as wrong.

According to the Mitchell translation, "The more prohibitions you have, / the less virtuous people will be" (57). More rules mean more rules to break or try to maneuver around. Rules are another way of trying to control events rather than to understand them.

Restrictions, weapons, tricks, and laws are all ways of confining the natural flow of events rather than allowing them to unfold, working with them through virtues rather than prohibitions. Let situations find their own levels, act in collaboration with the natural energies. Swimming upstream is always difficult.

The more weapons and tricks there are, the more likely that something will go wrong or someone will get hurt. As Mitchell puts it, "The more weapons you have, / the less secure people will be" (57). By allowing events to blossom according to nature, the leader helps establish an environment conducive to good work and virtuous activity.

Imagine that a new fad appears in school. Students wear a new-style watch which makes an annoying sound as each hour passes. As the principal, you create a new rule banning these watches. You empower staff to give students in violation of this new rule a detention on the spot. The problem only gets worse.

## "UNATTACHED ACTION"

Rather than trying to control the situation, the principal would do better to try to understand why students want to wear these watches and then work with the situation. New rules do not get at the underlying cause, or motivation, for the unwanted behavior. Working against the natural energy and flow of a situation rarely works.

Lao Tzu concludes this chapter with a direct statement of the actions that a leader should take:

> I let go of the law,
> and the people become honest.
> I let go of economics,
> and the people become prosperous.
> I let go of religion,
> and the people become serene.
> I let go of all desire for the common good,
> and the good becomes common as grass. (Mitchell 1988, 57)

Lin calls this "unattached action" (57). The successful leader, the leader who is a sage, does not become entangled with the world. She is dispassionate and objective. In this way, she can do the right thing, responding to the situation virtuously, and not from personal desires for control, power, wealth, praise, and the like.

The less the leader meddles, the better off everyone is. How long has it been since national and international market places simply reacted to events naturally rather than being controlled with rules, regulations, and artificial pricing?

As Sun Tzu tells us:

> [W]e know that the leader of the army is in charge of the lives of the people and the safety of the nation. (Cleary 1988, 31)

We could easily say this about the principal. The army becomes the staff and the nation the school. In the Denma Translation Group's version of Sun Tzu, they go so far as to characterize the leader as the "fate star" of the people (Denma Translation Group, 2001, 8). A principal is ultimately responsible for the welfare of the school and its inhabitants.

## POSITIVE RELATIONSHIPS

The effective principal does have to establish and maintain a positive relationship with the staff. She establishes an atmosphere of trust and goodwill. Sun Tzu knows how crucial this is.

> If soldiers are punished before a personal attachment to the leadership is formed, they will not submit, and if they do not submit they are hard to employ. (Cleary 1988, 130)

While humility in the leader is critical, she is still the leader and should not be afraid to lead overtly when the occasion calls for this. If positive relationships and trust have not been established, the principal will find it difficult to work with the staff. Through her actions, the principal must capture the faith of the people.

A leader should govern with a seriousness of purpose. According to Sun Tzu, one can be too nice, not holding people accountable to the purpose and vision of the school.

> If you are so nice to them that you cannot employ them, so kind to them that you cannot command them, so casual with them that you cannot establish order, they are like spoiled children, useless. (Cleary 1988, 138)

Trying to govern your friends is a tricky task; governing employees, even though you have good relations with them, is much easier. Governance is not a private activity. It involves the deliberate forging of relationships. The principal has to earn the trust, respect, and loyalty of the staff in order to govern successfully. Even when the leadership is subtle, not overt at all, positive human relationships must support the leader's governance.

## CHARACTERISTICS OF THE SAGE LEADER

In chapter 67 of the *Tao Te Ching*, Lao Tzu describes three characteristics of the sage leader: compassion, conservation, and not daring to be ahead in the world (Lin, 67).

Thus, the great leader cares deeply about others, does not waste anything, including action and energy, and remains humble. Being humble does not mean that the leader has completely no influence on the people. Sun Tzu writes, "If the army is unsettled, it means the general is not taken seriously" (Cleary 1988, 126). The principal is humble, not invisible.

Sun Tzu also understands the importance of compassion and relationship in any governance model:

> Look upon your soldiers as you do infants, and they willingly go into deep valleys with you; look upon your soldiers as beloved children, and they willingly die with you. (Cleary 1988, 137)

This is not to say that the leadership infantilizes members of the organization. The metaphor suggests that the leadership handles people with the same compassion and care that one would one's own children, tough love, doing what is in the people's best interest because the leader cares about them.

Through these three characteristics, a leader or principal can establish powerful ties with the staff. Having built these connections between himself and the staff, he can count on the staff being with him.

Clearly then, Taoism teaches a leader to be self-effacing, not lordly. If one chooses to flow with the Tao, then naturally there will be little flurry. The leader will not oppose the natural order of things, and she will not call attention to herself. The great leader works quietly with the natural energy flow around her. The task of the general/principal is very clear according to Sun Tzu:

> Thus one advances without seeking glory, retreats without avoiding blame, only protecting people to the benefit of the government as well, thus rendering valuable service to the nation. (Cleary 1988, 137)

Recall the discussion of favor and disgrace above. Commenting on *The Art of War*, the eleventh-century Chinese scholar Wang Xi noted that "Skillful warriors are able to allow the force of momentum to seize victory for them without exerting their strength" (Cleary 1988, 67). The idea of working with existing energies and using only minimal exertion is central to the leadership as envisioned by both Lao Tzu and Sun Tzu.

Fighting against the tide of events is exhausting and often ineffective. If the staff wants change, and the principal offers stagnation, trouble will ensue. The wise principal would take advantage of the staff's desire for change to effect the changes that he wants.

Humility is a central aspect of the sage's character. We so often associate leadership with power and the grandiose. However, the Tao teaches quite the opposite. A principal should know his limits, when and when not to impose himself onto a situation.

The less the leader interferes, the better. He accepts his people as they are and respects them. So do principals have to deal with many different people, always being respectful and decorous. Leaders do not judge; they simply act intelligently and virtuously based on what is before them. They accept the many points of view of the staff with respect.

Their goal is to deal with the world as a unified whole which has natural directions and energies. Working with, as opposed to doing to, is the order of the day (Lin 2006, 72).

The idea of respect also applies to working with one's adversaries. A principal has to confront many people and organizations, especially the staff, which may or may not agree with him. Sometimes the disagreement can be antagonistic and even bitter. A good leader always respects his opponent and treats him or her with dignity. He knows that there is merit in everyone's ideas, and considers all ideas.

Sun Tzu says that "A surrounded enemy must be given a way out" (Cleary 1988, 108). In other words, the principal, once having won his position, should leave a way out for those who have lost the argument to leave with dignity. Allow them to back away quietly, even using some of their ideas in the final solution.

These staff members should not be made to feel foolish or inadequate or wrong. In this way, those in opposition do not feel shamed, outcast, or disregarded. A good leader wants to be able to count on these people another day.

Sun Tzu also says, "Do not press a desperate enemy" (Cleary 1988, 108). There is no need to crush the opposition. People who are cornered and feeling desperate are apt to strike out, perhaps irrationally. Throwing your victory in the face of others only makes people feel anger and resentment.

Instead, by gently backing away after achieving her goals, the effective leader is respectful and appreciative of those who did not get their way. She sincerely thanks them for their participation in the decision process. Again, this will help ensure their continued loyalty in the future.

## READING THE SITUATION—FLEXIBILITY

Effective principals must be flexible, ready to adapt their actions and strategies to the situation, not try to force old or inappropriate strategies onto a unique set of circumstances. According to Sun Tzu, "[V]ictory in war is not repetitious, but adapts its form endlessly" (Cleary 1988, 93).

Just because a strategy worked in the past does not guarantee its success in the present. Every situation is in some way unique, defined by its own special characteristics. The wise principal examines a situation fully before choosing a course of action.

Sun Tzu compares this flexibility to a characteristic of water:

> So a military force has no constant formation, water has no constant shape: the ability to gain victory by changing and adapting according to the opponent is called genius. (Cleary 1988, 94)

The successful principal reads a situation before deciding how to respond. He does not proceed as if he has seen this situation before. Instead, he analyzes what is happening, who he is dealing with, his own resources, and then confronts or works with what is happening. A former incident may inform a current one, but the two are rarely, if ever, exactly the same.

Acting without first fully understanding the situation leads to failure.

When a leader repeatedly "gets it" wrong, people begin to drift away, placing their confidence elsewhere. The great leader approaches each situation with the same virtue and skill, but not with the same action. She sees the value in adapting her actions to fit the specifics of the moment.

Even if one is skilled at reading situations, that knowledge is useless unless the leader applies it in choosing a course of action. Sun Tzu says,

> Therefore generals who know all possible adaptations to take advantage of the ground know how to use military force. If generals do not know how to adapt advantageously, even if they know the lay of the land they cannot take advantage of it.
>
> If they rule armies without knowing the arts of complete adaptivity, they cannot get people to work for them, even if they know what there is to gain, they cannot get people to work for them. (Cleary 1988, 111)

In the same way, the leader has to be flexible yet resolute in accepting all the people, not judging or advancing one person's ideas over those of another. In chapter 49 of the *Tao Te Ching*, Lao Tzu writes:

> The sages have no constant mind.
> They take the mind of the people as their mind.
> Those who are good, I am good to them.
> Those who are not good, I am also good to them.
> Thus the virtue of goodness.
> Those who believe, I believe them.
> Those who do not believe, I also believe them.
> Thus the virtue of belief. (Lin 2006, 49)

The constants are goodness and belief. The successful leader shows flexibility by accepting the ideas and actions of everyone without compromising the virtues of goodness and belief. All people should be treated with goodness, as the leader demonstrates. The beliefs of everyone are worth considering as valid, as the successful leader also demonstrates. There is good in everyone. The Mitchell translation calls this "true goodness" and "true trust" (49).

Another aspect of flexibility is preparedness. If the leader is prepared for dangerous events, then she can anticipate them and meet them successfully head-on. In fact, the best way to deal with difficulties may actually be to avoid them. According to Sun Tzu,

> So the rule of military operations is not to count on opponents not coming, but to rely on having ways of dealing with them; not to count on opponents not attacking, but to rely on having what cannot be attacked. (Cleary 1988, 113–14)

Thus, there are two kinds of preparedness. First, one must always be ready for the unexpected. This means to understand the dangers that may exist and plan for them. It may also mean to find ways to avoid them or prevent them from ever occurring.

"That which cannot be attacked" can be a program or argument that is so well constructed that attacks fall by the wayside as ineffective. In fact, people may not even attempt to attack. Think of the example above in which the leader needed a solid rationale when distributing limited resources.

Another way to be protected is by having a character beyond reproach. Such a character cannot be assailed effectively. Those attacking such a character will appear ignorant and ill advised. The effective administrator takes the moral high ground as well as preparing a defense to use in the event of an attack. He has his ducks in a row.

## BETWEEN THE STAFF AND THE BOARD

The principal stands between the staff and the school board. She is a buffer, hopefully protecting individuals from board members who want to micromanage the school, thus interfering with the governance structure the principal and staff have developed. Sun Tzu speaks to this situation when he describes how the civil leadership can interfere with the operation of the army:

> When a civil leadership unaware of the facts tells its armies to advance when it should not, or tells its armies to retreat when it should not, this is called tying up the armies. When the civil leadership is ignorant of military affairs but

shares equally in the government of the armies, the soldiers get confused. When the civil leadership is ignorant of military maneuvers but shares equally in the command of the armies, the soldiers hesitate. (Cleary 1988, 49)

How many times does a principal have to shield the staff from unreasonable or unnecessary directives from the board, or even a single board member? The principal is on the line and knows what is happening. Part of his task is to deal with educational issues. That was what his training was about. The role of the board is leadership through policy development.

The principal is the leader immediately on the ground, the person who should be empowered to take charge on a day-to-day basis. Otherwise, as Sun Tzu tells us,

Once the armies are confused and hesitant, trouble comes from competitors. This is called taking away victory by deranging the military. (Cleary 1988, 50)

Perhaps the board decides that all teachers should always have their next three weeks of lesson plans on record with the principal. In addition, they require the principal to review those plans and submit a summary report to the board every three weeks.

What the board does not know is that lessons are fluid, constantly changing in response to what is happening, the teachable moment, a snow day, or a special event. Teachers do not have the time to plan three weeks in advance. What is the purpose of the principal's reading all of these plans?

The principal's job is now to inform the board, to teach them about how teachers and schools work on a day-to-day basis. He must make them understand that their requests are not fully reasonable and will interfere with the operation of the school, as well as have deleterious effect on staff morale.

He could offer a counter suggestion. Maybe teachers could submit their *last* three weeks of plans, and the principal would then write a brief summary of anything outstanding or unusual he finds in those plans.

He also knows the difficulty he can expect in informing the teachers of this new directive. He will hear many reasons why this is simply not feasible and not educationally sound. The teachers will expect the good principal to represent their thoughts and opinions at board meetings. There is a good chance that the principal will lose some credibility if he cannot somehow ameliorate the situation.

If a leader, in this case the principal, is not free to perform the duties of the job, there is no telling how a situation will turn out. If a principal is to provide governance, then the system must allow the principal to govern.

## CASE STUDY 1

*Your school has decided to experiment with a shared governance model. The staff has elected seven teachers to serve on the faculty council, charged with collaborating with the administration in running the school. The council is not an advisory group. Rather, it is an actual force in the decision making process. As the principal, you are going to have to collaborate with this group, sharing your authority and power.*

*You quickly realize that the faculty council has a different idea of collaboration than you do. They see your opinion, or vote, as one of eight votes in deciding issues. Obviously, that means that you have been reduced to 12.5 percent of the governing process, and can be outvoted easily.*

*The reality of the situation is that the teachers do not really want to share. They want to control such areas as hiring (but not firing), professional evaluation, schedules, budget proposals, and the like. They are happy to leave the daily operation of the school to you, under their ultimate control.*

*You have to walk a tightrope. On the one hand you do not want to appear against the idea of the staff and principal collaborating on important decisions. However, there are some serious flaws with the system as proposed. The first area of concern is responsibility.*

*Let's say that your school is understaffed. However, the council votes to give every teacher a second planning period. You know that this will not work, cannot be done under the present circumstances. Ultimately you are outvoted. The council goes ahead with a plan to add planning periods to the day at the expense of classroom and special class time (art, music, physical education, health).*

*The school board is furious. Who are they going to hold responsible for this mess? You. You are the ultimate authority in the school, a licensed principal hired to run the operation. The faculty council can walk away from the situation, but you cannot. On the other hand, the council members are heroes to the staff for coming up with and implementing this idea. The board cannot really put the blame on the faculty council, because you are in charge.*

*There are other issues. You are licensed to evaluate teachers. The council is not. You have the authority and experience to create a workable student schedule. The other council members do not. You can already see that there are going to be proposed changes which will not work, which will fail, leaving you to pick up the pieces. What are you going to do?*

1. What have you learned about governance in this chapter that you can apply to the case study?
2. How will you approach this governance problem?

3. Will you involve the school board?
4. How will you maintain positive relations with the staff?
5. How can you use staff ideas in you proposed solution?
6. What is your solution?
7. What are the forces and energies flowing through this situation?
8. How will you assert your authority without becoming an autocrat?

## CASE STUDY 2

*Recently in the national news there have been several stories about armed intruders entering schools. This has led to intense conversations, including staff, school administrators, school board members, parents, students, and the community in general. Your phone is ringing off the hook with concerned parents. Some of them are threatening, demanding that you take action.*

*Two ideas have emerged from all of this talk. One is that everyone who works in the school should wear photo ID. While this proposal has gained some traction, people hold strong opinions both for and against it. You are going to have to deal with this. A more volatile proposal, also gaining some traction, is that an armed, plain-clothed police officer always be on campus.*

*Interestingly, the most prominent staff member in favor of the ID idea is a teacher who always supports and helps you. You can rely on her whenever you are in a tough spot. The leader of the group that sees the ID idea as reflective of a prison environment and possibly a constitutional issue is the president of the teachers' union. None of the staff is in favor of the policeman idea.*

*You abhor violence. You have never hunted, shot a gun, or owned a gun. In fact, you served in the military as a conscientious objector doing clerical work. The school community is divided on gun control, and many people hunt. There is a large percentage of the population that knows about and understands guns and gun safety. Could a police presence be a good way to go? There is definitely some community support for this idea.*

*You are balancing a delicate combination of safety, restriction, and danger. The local police force has offered to help fund the officer-on-campus idea. The board is interested in this possibility, but it is also hotly divided over the gun. They would readily accept a police officer with no gun.*

*How does the fact that your daughter and the children of your neighbors attend this school, affect your thinking?*

*The situation will test not only your ability to make collaborative decisions, but also the nature of your governance style. Are you collaborative? Are you autocratic? Are you influenced by those you trust and those you don't? Do you govern from your heart and beliefs?*

*The school board has asked you to develop a plan of action on this issue at the end of two months.*

1. Which aspects of governance, as developed in this chapter, can you apply to this situation?
2. Where will you go for advice?
3. What is your plan for gathering information?
4. What is your plan for hearing all voices?
5. What are your priorities: student safety, weapons in school, teacher satisfaction?
6. How will you work with those teachers and community members who do not get their way?
7. How will your governance style affect the outcome in this case?
8. Do you need a particular governance style to best ensure that the decision-making process will go well? If so, what would that look like?

*Chapter Three*

# When to Act and When Not to Act

### WU WEI

There is a concept in Taoism called "wu wei." This

> is the non-doing that leaves nothing undone. Non-doing, therefore, refers to that doing which does not require one to use effort. It is not forcing things to happen. It is doing that seeks to flow along with the flow of nature itself. (Sorajjakool 2001, 92)

We are often impatient. We see a problem or we see that events are not going our way. We want to jump in and fix things. That is leadership, is it not? We have a difficult time tolerating ambiguity. We want to do something, get involved, show that we can deal with the situation. Action is seen as better than passivity. Yet sometimes it might be wiser to allow circumstances to work themselves out.

Chapter 63 of the Lin translation of the *Tao Te Ching* suggests that a leader does what needs to be done without actually doing anything (127). Lao Tzu is telling the reader not to become too enmeshed in situations. He argues for a light touch.

A leader can do without doing by literally doing nothing, allowing a situation to play out and resolve itself. If two colleagues are having a dispute, rather than meddling right away as the peacemaker, the wise leader might choose to wait to learn more about the situation and watch what develops. The two individuals may very well resolve their differences without the leader's help.

# Chapter 3
# THE CHOICE NOT TO ACT

Not doing is not simply inaction because you do not know what to do or cannot do what is required. It is deliberately not acting, not imposing your will on events. This can be very difficult to do, especially when we think we have the answer or things are not going our way. Staff expects the principal to act, to solve things. Not doing takes great patience and courage.

If the principal can understand the natural rhythms and energies of a situation, then working with those forces rather than trying to control them, will often be more successful. Do you try to implement a new policy which 95 percent of the faculty, students, and parents oppose, or do you find another way to solve the problem?

A major risk of nonaction is the perception that the leader is doing nothing. This results in political fallout and lack of confidence from the staff. We expect our leaders to do something about every situation or issue. Rarely does it occur to us that doing nothing might be the wisest course of action. This is why nonaction takes courage. Subordinates want their leaders to solve every problem, thus alleviating themselves of responsibility.

> To accept our ignorance is to be opened. When one is opened one can see things more clearly because one has ceased to impose the cognitive category of "what life ought to be" on being and allow being to speak for itself. To allow being to speak to us is to allow it to reveal itself. "Being" reveals itself when we stop trying to force "being" into a certain mode of being but allow the self to experience that which is and through this "isness" come to understand the self. (Sorajjakool 2001, 92–93)

## CONTROL

It is our nature to want to control the environment around us. However, as noted above, and in previous chapters, this book addresses the idea of working with natural energies and forces, not trying to channel them against the current. We have to be patient and hold back trying to impose our values and attitudes on reality, allowing reality to express itself. The *Tao Te Ching* warns us that trying to control the world will inevitably fail (Lin 2006, 59).

We are not as powerful, big, or sacred as the world. It is for us to learn from, not to control. Trying to control the world is like trying to control a nuclear explosion. The concept is absurd. Rather, we are to respect the world, hold it in awe, and learn from it. We must educate ourselves to understand the actions, forces, and systems of the world without interference. Only by using that knowledge can we hope to work with natural circumstances and do what is right (Lin 2006, 59).

If the dress code does not work, pushing harder on compliance probably will not work either. Discover why students will not comply, and then work with what you discover.

For instance, hats often present a problem in schools. Traditionally, one does not wear a hat in school. Yet, current fashion makes hats important. Rather than rowing against this tide, trying to eliminate hats, the principal would probably do better to limit hats to certain styles and specific situations. For instance, the principal might allow baseball style caps, but not worn backwards. They must also not interfere with the teachers' seeing student faces.

Wang Xi, an eleventh-century Chinese scholar commenting on *The Art of War*, wrote:

> Skillful warriors are able to allow the force of momentum to seize victory for them without exerting their strength. (Cleary 1988, 67)

If one can understand the situation deeply, overt action may not be necessary to resolve the situation successfully. Better to work with the world than against it.

According to Lao Tzu:

> Take the world by constantly applying noninterference
> The one who interferes is not qualified to take the world (Lin 2006, 97)

Once again, the point is to interfere as little as possible in a situation as opposed to working with the conditions one finds.

## STEPPING BACK

Imagine that the school board has passed a new directive. Any student who is absent from school cannot participate in extracurricular activities on that same day. You are not so sure that this is a good idea, but you resist jumping into the middle of it. You do not lobby the board either way. You explain the situation to the staff, but you do not take sides. Instead, you listen to what teachers have to say, and take this under advisement.

Knowing that this idea will upset many coaches, activity directors, and parents, you sit back and allow things to happen. As you thought, many complaints start coming in. No one seems to be happy. You tell all those who complain that their only recourse it to speak to the board. Board members start receiving calls. Thirty people attend the next board meeting, speaking against the new rule. The board will still have the last word, but they will likely reverse the policy.

You have allowed circumstances to work themselves out. You could have spoken to the entire board or to individual board members to try to convince them one way or the other. You might have mobilized those in favor of the idea or those against the idea, and helped them decide what to say to the board.

You have realized that you cannot change the situation. You cannot impose your will on the board or change the directive. You have a feeling that the board will rescind the action if enough parents and lead teachers protest. However, by not taking sides, you are not in a conflict for or against anyone's position. You do not alienate the board.

In the end, what happens is a result of allowing the situation to work itself out, and your understanding of the likely direction things will take. In time, hopefully, people will see your nonaction as wisdom and not simply as shirking your duty.

## ACT EARLY

Chapter 64 of the *Tao Te Ching* begins this way:

> It is easy to hold
> what is still stable.
> It is easy to mold
> what is not yet formed.
> It is easy to shatter
> what is still fragile.
> It is easy to scatter
> what is yet light and small.
> Therefore, act now rather than wait.
> Get things done before it's too late. (Dale 2002, 129)

Leading is easy when everything is going well, when there is stability. Fragile and small things are subject to direction by you. However, once the situation changes, the principal will have a more difficult job on his hands.

If you have to act, act at the earliest possible moment, before everything gets too complicated. If a bullying problem is beginning to emerge in your school, you need to correct it at soon as you can. If you wait, the problem will spread and be much more difficult to control. Fix a leak while it is small. Don't wait for gushing water!

As the Mitchell translation says:

> Prevent trouble before it arises.
> Put things in order before they exist. (Mitchell 1988, 64)

Acting before there is a problem is the best of all. Inspect the plumbing and shore up any weak spots. Make sure there are enough supplies so teachers will not have to compete with each other to get things first. Avoid the problems all together. Before a principal implements a new policy, she would be wise to work with the staff around the issues the policy is created to address. Correct any misconceptions and calm any fears before the situation can get out of hand.

Taking small actions before situations get out of hand will avoid more complicated situations later on. The passage suggests that one become involved only so much as is necessary and allow natural forces to develop unencumbered.

If the principal analyzes situations carefully, she may be able to anticipate events, knowing what will lead to what. In this case, she takes the time to prepare before anything actually happens. Acting before the event or situation develops can be more important than what the principal does after events are under way.

## BE PREPARED

Sun Tzu tells us:

> Take three months to prepare your machine and three months to complete your siege engineering. (Cleary 1988, 39)

Half a year of preparation is better than having to deal with chaotic conditions. Also, careful planning can minimize damage and destruction. By reading the natural energies and forces of a situation, the successful leader can anticipate what will happen and where various events will lead, and thus, as seen elsewhere, win the battle before it begins. If the leader has sufficiently prepared the ground, when the event occurs, he may have to do nothing but watch things work themselves out.

Perhaps the principal has decided that students cannot leave the building during the day. However, the building has twenty-two doors, and they must remain unlocked due to fire regulations. Trying to keep students in will be a hopeless endeavor.

The principal might want to prepare certain aspects of the situation before implementation of the new rule. He could call the fire marshal to see if some of the doors could be locked. He could assign staff to watch the doors most likely to be used. He may decide that the best course of action is to have people outside to watch for students. The principal may actually discover that the situation is untenable, and instead of the proposed policy, work out the details of a safe, open campus.

## KNOW YOURSELF AND BE PATIENT

Besides careful preparation before action, knowing oneself and one's resources is critical. Sun Tzu observes:

> So there are five ways of knowing who will win. Those who know when to fight and when not to fight are victorious. Those who discern when to use many or few troops are victorious. Those whose upper and lower ranks have the same desire are victorious. Those who face the unprepared with preparation are victorious. Those whose generals are able and are not constrained by their governments are victorious. These are the five ways to know who will win. (Cleary 1988, 51)

The principal in the situation above (students not allowed to leave the school), realizing that her initial plan will not work, might explain the facts and problems to the faculty, gather information that way, and assign a group of teachers the task of coming up with two or three solutions. This could avoid a lot of difficulty and frustration.

Knowing when and when not to act is vital to success. For instance, a principal might assume that teachers are going to balk at implementing the new dress code. He spends hours preparing a campaign to ensure success of the new regulations. A representative of the faculty asks to speak with him about the new code.

Anticipating the worst, the principal immediately begins to challenge the teacher, only to find out that her message is that the faculty is behind the measure but just wants clarification on a few matters. Do not jump to action. Take in the whole situation first.

## THE USE OF FORCE

Lao Tzu says that "Ruling a large country is like cooking a small fish" (Lin 2006, 121). If the cook meddles too much with the fish, it will fall apart. Poking, turning, moving the fish more than necessary will ruin it. It is the same with leading a school. Do not interfere with the affairs of the institution or its members more than is necessary. Act when you have to and be patient at other times.

Similarly, the leader needs to know when to use more or less force, if she uses any force at all. Do you need a sledgehammer to drive a pushpin? Perhaps the principal wants to control the chaotic student behaviors in the hallways between classes.

She demands that every teacher and paraprofessional be in the halls for the entire passing period. All administrators must be in the halls at the same time. There will be cameras in all general areas to monitor and record behavior. She has brought in several parent volunteers to increase supervision. Or, perhaps the cameras are enough. There may not be the need for Draconian methods.

Being unified and prepared are two crucial aspects of knowing when to act. Trying to implement a new program when a large percentage of the staff is solidly opposed will most likely result in conflict and avoidance. Teachers may simply not enforce the dress code if they so choose. Forcing them to do what they oppose will not be easy, and it will lead to ill will, winners and losers, power struggles, and confusion for students and parents.

## AVOIDING CONFLICT

This would be an example of failing to act in advance. The principal has to sell the idea first, or he may find himself a paper tiger, trying to enforce a rule with no support.

According to Sun Tzu:

> Therefore the victories of good warriors are not noted for cleverness or bravery. Therefore their victories in battle are not flukes. Their victories are not flukes because they position themselves where they will surely win, prevailing over those who have already lost. (Cleary 1988, 62)

The proper action, then, is to act before something happens, not making up the plan in the middle of the action. If the leader carefully starts in the right place, then he has a much better chance of success. The principal and board would be wise to talk to as many people as possible, get a sense of where everyone stands, and then decide whether or not to increase graduation requirements.

There are those who say that they love a good fight. According to the *Tao Te Ching,* this is a dangerous philosophy.

> The military is a tool of misfortune
> All things detest it
> Therefore, those who possess the Tao avoid it . . .
> When using it [the military] out of necessity
> Calm detachment should be above all
> Victorious but without glory
> Those who glorify
> Are delighting in the killing
> Those who delight in killing

Cannot achieve their ambitions upon the world (Lin 2006, 63)

Thus, a principal avoids conflict. He does not relish it. When a difference of opinion arises, the principal's job is to try everything else before resorting to some sort of fight or showdown. Destroying your enemy simply encourages enmity and fear. Conflict breeds conflict.

It would be better to convert your enemy and bring him to your side rather than leave him humiliated and cut off. Respect the other side. You may need that enemy later on another occasion. This is a vicious cycle where everyone eventually loses.

Lao Tzu explains the actions of a good leader after the conflict as well (Lin, 61). Engaging in conflict is destructive to both sides. A principal will have to work with those with whom he has been in conflict. They are most likely teachers or parents or board members who are not going away. There is no need to alienate them any further by crushing them or bragging. The good leader does only what is absolutely necessary when there is no choice but to engage in conflict.

## THE MEANS TO ACT

Principals need to have the latitude to act. They have to do what they see as necessary without being micromanaged by a higher authority. How can they plan if they have to have approval for everything they do? How can they act on the spot as needed if they do not have the authority to do so? Too many school boards see their role as running the school, when they should be working in the realm of policy

Even though Sun Tzu said, "In ancient times skillful warriors first made themselves invincible, and then watched for vulnerability in their opponents" (Cleary, 55), he also said that "[V]ictory can be discerned but not manufactured" (Cleary, 57). In other words, nothing is guaranteed. One cannot create a successful situation if there is simply nothing going in the necessary direction.

Here, too, is the problem with arrogance or inflated self-value. Having too much confidence in yourself can lead to carelessness and blindness.

No matter how much the principal plans, there is always a risk whenever he acts. Doing starts a series of events in motion. You cannot always anticipate how tenacious or strong an opponent's beliefs will be. You may think you have more support than you do. You may stir up conflict and resistance if you are not careful. Events have a life of their own. Once you make a commitment, you cannot take it back.

One should heed the advice of Sun Tzu:

Therefore the considerations of the intelligent always include both benefit and harm. As they consider benefit, their work can expand; as they consider harm, their troubles can be resolved. (Cleary 1988, 113)

## AVOID HARMING OTHERS AND YOURSELF

Do as much good as possible. Do as little harm as you can. This brings us back to not doing. Once you decide to act, there is no turning back. Before you act, the possibilities are endless. There are many actions you can take, many paths you can choose to follow. Once you commit, this infinite potential is gone. Thus, not doing until you fully understand a situation allows you to watch matters unfold before you decide on an action, if indeed you choose to act at all.

Imagine some hopeless battles. Perhaps you want to recommend cutting the sports program as a cost-saving measure. However, the school is in a town where sports are highly valued. Maybe you want to save Latin, although the enrollment this year was only ten students in grades 9 through 12. The board sees an unnecessary position where you see a fundamental subject to hold on to for your future students. Sun Tzu warns:

> There are routes not to be followed, armies not to be attacked, citadels not to be besieged, territory not to be fought over, orders of civilian governments not to be obeyed. (Cleary 1988, 110)

The advice then is to pick your battles. Why waste the energy on a confrontation which you cannot win? On the other hand, you may feel so strongly about your position that you cannot leave the situation alone and feel that it is your duty to confront those who oppose you. At least you know what you are getting into and do so deliberately.

## A TAOIST APPROACH

Knowing when and how much to act is a delicate matter. The Western tendency is to jump right into the fray, to get into the action. The Taoist way is more contemplative and reflective. This is not to say that one method is unilaterally superior to the other. However, a good leader knows the difference between a situation which calls for action and one which calls for noninterference.

Holding back when you believe you know what to do is difficult. Think back to the example of the teacher who wrote long memos. The natural response would be to answer the memo. However, answering the memo only brought another, even longer letter.

But, isn't the polite, professional action for a principal to answer the questions and complaints of a staff member? Examining the situation after the first few exchanges reveals the pattern. Respond to a memo and receive a more complex memo.

Working with this analysis, the answer becomes obvious. Break the cycle by doing nothing, and the memos will stop. Not doing is the way to work with this situation. That is, not failing to do what should be done or not knowing what to do and how to do it, but deliberately not doing. Knowing what to do, how to do it, and when to not do is the challenge for the educational leader.

## CASE STUDY 1

*A book in the school library has come under attack by some parents because it contains content which they think is inappropriate for young children. They have called you, the principal, to ask that you remove the book. You have told them that you will have to think about this before taking any action. They are temporarily satisfied.*

*You have bought some time. You begin to research censorship, find out which organizations will help you, and how to contact the American Civil Liberties Union. Your 1960s-era college years are in full swing as you bridle at this imposition on the rights of people being able to choose what they want to read.*

*After about three weeks, you have amassed a great deal of information. You are ready for the battle. You have at least twenty hours into this. The parents are no longer willing to wait for your response, so they have contacted the board to be put on the agenda of the next meeting.*

*Meanwhile, you have been having conversations with various staff members you think will agree with your opinion. Your goal is to have a good number of teachers at the meeting opposing any kind of censorship in the school. You have also gathered community members sympathetic to your cause.*

*The day of the meeting arrives. Twenty teachers and community members who support you are there. Surprisingly, there are about ten citizens there who would like to see the book banned. The grumbling has started even before the meeting begins.*

*The agenda item comes up, and several people on the board and in the audience ask to be heard. Debate goes on for about a half hour, and tempers are beginning to get hot. You are trying to skate a thin line between the two groups, but your leaning is clear. You don't want to appear as if you don't care, and you also want to avoid looking like a hypocrite.*

*One particular board member, who usually remains quiet, signals that he has something to say. Holding up the board policy manual, he cites policy B24, "Review of Instructional Materials." It lays out a procedure for reviewing materials that parents or other community members find objectionable.*

*The policy calls for the formation of a committee: the principal, a board member, two teachers, the complainant, and two additional community members. Their charge is to review the material in question and decide its fate, by majority vote if necessary. The decision of this committee is then ratified by the full board, merely a formality at that point.*

*The committee is to be formed within the next week and report three weeks after that.*

1. What ideas from this chapter could you apply to this situation?
2. Were your actions justified?
3. What could be some of the results of talking to so many people ahead of time?
4. How might you have acted more effectively?
5. What possible damage might you have done to your reputation?
6. Who would have made sense to talk to first?
7. Were the twenty hours of preparation well spent? How else could you have spent it?
8. How will you look if the decision goes your way? If it does not go your way?

## CASE STUDY 2

*You, the principal of a large elementary school, know that the board wants to cut positions to control the budget. When they see small classes, they see unnecessary staff. Their tendency is to look at the number of students a teacher works with and not what that teacher does. For instance, the art teacher works with every student in the school. The special-education teacher may work with only six students.*

*Teachers are coming to you to present the reasons why they should be renewed. Parents are calling every day defending their favorite teachers. Those interested in sports call to defend teachers who coach.*

*The board wants you to suggest which positions should be done away with. The decisions, obviously, are extremely difficult. Some of these teachers are old friends. Some are mediocre. Some are exceptional. You sense that the board is going to go after the special-education teachers, each with only ten students. You cannot afford to lose these teachers, especially if that means teachers in oversized classes will have to make more accommodations.*

*You are not sure where to cut, but you know where you cannot. Virtually the whole staff agrees that they could not function without the three special-education teachers. People are wondering why you are not doing more to save this group. They are concerned about your inaction.*

*What they do not know is that you have spoken to some key board members about the situation. Appearing to favor one teacher over another would be disastrous. You have convinced the board members to keep the special-education teachers. As for further recommendations, you supply the board with a chart showing how many students each teacher has, what he or she teaches, who runs extracurricular activities, and the number of students in each year, grades 1 through 6.*

*In particular, the special education teachers are unhappy with your not making more of a public case for their positions. They do not know the subtleties of the situation. What you are doing is very delicate. You want to go into the decision process without pitting one teacher against another. Showing favorites would not be helpful. It would only inflame the situation. You have managed to secure what you need before the decision is ever made, and you have provided significant information to the board.*

*In the end, the losses to the school are confined to one teacher, two paraprofessionals, field trips, and several maintenance projects.*

1. Whicht concepts from this chapter can you apply to this situation?
2. Was it wise to keep your strategy secret from the staff? Is this dishonest?
3. How else could you have handled the situation?
4. Describe the natural energies and forces of the situation.
5. When should you act, and when should you not act? How should you act?
6. Have you played favorites with the special-education staff?
7. Is it all right to set up an outcome with the board before the actual action?
8. How did you set the ground for success, or at least to cut your losses?
9. Which aspects of your reputation and ability to govern were at stake in this situation? Do you think you did the right thing with respect to that issue?

*Chapter Four*

# Power Struggles and Conflicts

### ALL KINDS OF CONFLICTS

A common problem for leaders is the power struggle. What do you do if someone will not do what you say, even if you think it is a reasonable request within the person's job description? How do you overcome basic resistance? Is there a way to do this without feeling petty and nasty?

Power struggles are only one type of conflict. Decisions, budgets, student discipline, parent complaints, and unpopular directives all involve conflict. Are there reasonable and successful ways of dealing with conflict without succumbing to it?

A power struggle necessarily involves at least two sides. Generally, there is a lot of head butting, and victory can be more a result of persistence and obstinacy than of any logical thought or strategy. A power struggle is just that, a conflict to see who has more power, a bullfight. However, one of the two parties can simply refuse to engage. As Sun Tzu says:

> When you do not want to do battle, even if you draw a line on the ground to hold, the opponent cannot fight with you because you set him off on the wrong track. (Cleary 1988, 84)

### DRESS-CODE VIOLATION

A teacher sends a female high school student to the office for a dress-code violation. The student dresses in a counterculture style. She has many layers of clothing, some ripped, all in different colors. The problem, as the principal sees it, is that there are areas where too much flesh is exposed.

The student is ready for a fight, thinking that the school does not like her clothing because it is different. She is used to being misunderstood or not valued, so her expectations of this encounter are clear before she ever gets to the office. The principal completely disarms her by complimenting her outfit, telling her that it is delightful with so many colors and textures.

She does not know what to say. Her assumptions fall flat. Then when the principal says that some of the clothing is too exposing, she readily understands and is willing to cover up. There is no battle, no struggle, no anger. The principal has upheld the dress code without a fight. The student has encountered a pleasant attitude she was not prepared for, and thus felt more comfortable being cooperative.

Imagine a power struggle as two individuals' hands clasped and pulling in opposite directions. By letting go, one party can end the struggle. In other words, refuse to accept the struggle as the only way to resolution.

According to chapter 22 of the *Tao Te Ching*, one should

> Yield and remain whole,
> Bend and remain straight. (Lin 2006, 48)

In any conflict, a leader is likely to be reduced. Anger, revenge, insult all take away something from one's character. To remain whole, in other words to keep your dignity and professionalism, it is best to remain flexible, yielding. A leader can withstand being argued with, yelled at, even insulted. Let the other vent while remaining calm. Keep yourself whole. When the other is done, you can respond with thoughtfulness and dignity. Yield while at the same time being faithful to your beliefs.

## THE CONTENTIOUS IEP MEETING

At a contentious individualized education program (IEP) meeting, the principal had to be very careful with the student's mother, who was very angry at what she perceived as a misunderstanding and consequent mistreatment of her daughter. The principal knew what was coming and had prepared himself for the "battle" which would inevitably occur. He had a strategy.

At the end of the meeting, the only individuals left in the room were the school psychologist, the mother, the mother's advocate, and the principal. The principal's strategy was to allow the mom to vent, no matter how bad the situation became. Indeed, she then began to insult the principal, calling him stupid, even knocking his head lightly with her hand to indicate his lack of brains.

The principal never admitted to wrongdoing. Instead, he made statements like, "I am sorry that I made you and your daughter feel bad." He was betting that she would hear these words as an admission of having done something wrong and feel satisfied. After about fifteen minutes of this abuse, the mother finally left.

That is the last time the principal ever heard from the mother. She had satisfied her need to express her anger, particularly at the principal. Had he tried to reason with her, or argue in his own defense, there is no telling what might have happened. He was no worse for having been insulted, and the situation at school returned to a fragile normalcy. People may not have left the room happy, but they all had attained some sense of satisfaction. Give away the victory and take the defeat, as the Buddhist would say.

The successful leader will avoid those actions which might incite others, resulting in conflict. Avoiding conflict altogether is the best way of dealing with it. Once the situation is resolved to the principal's satisfaction, then she stops, not pressing her position to the point where others are insulted, demeaned, or angered.

## DO NOT OVERDO

> A good commander achieves results, then stops
> And does not dare to reach for domination
> Achieves result but does not brag
> Achieves result but does not flaunt
> Achieves result but is not arrogant
> Achieves result but only out of necessity
> Achieves result but does not dominate. (Lin 2006, 61)

If one has to fight, then so be it. However, it is wise not to push any further than is absolutely necessary. This will either prolong the conflict or cause new conflicts to arise. Remember the teacher who had to have the last word through answering every memo with another memo. There is no need to try to actually silence that person.

The Mitchell translation says, "The master does his job / and then stops" (30). Suppose you were working with a teacher with whom you had a real personality conflict. He asks you for some time off, but you believe that this particular time will unduly inconvenience the school. You deny the request at a meeting with this individual. The teacher has a lot to say about your decision.

You listen quietly, not entering into the conflict unnecessarily. When he is done, you explain your decision calmly. Then, when you are finished saying what you need to, the teacher requests some extra materials for his classroom. You are tempted to deny this request as well, just to teach him a lesson. However, you realize that such a move on your part is not only motivated by the desire to punish, but also will result in further, needless conflict.

Lao Tzu sees avoiding conflict from the start as the best strategy. Battle, or in our case conflict, is a last resort. Even then, conflict should be used in a detached manner. The principal should not enjoy the fight. Furthermore, she should not view victory as a glorious event. Battle must be seen as a necessity when it cannot be avoided, never as something to relish and enter into with excitement over the challenge. (Lin, 63)

As the Mitchell translation puts the issue:

> He enters into battle gravely,
> with sorrow and with great compassion,
> as if he were attending a funeral. (31)

In this translation, Lao Tzu reminds the leader that

> His enemies are not demons,
> but human beings like himself.
> He doesn't wish them personal harm
> nor does he rejoice in victory. (31)

Taking satisfaction and enjoyment in conflict is simply not a good idea.

## AVOIDABLE OR UNAVOIDABLE CONFLICT

However, if a principal must enter into a conflict, then she should be prepared to win quickly and with the least loss on either side. Zhang Yu, commenting on *The Art of War* during the Sung Dynasty, tells us:

> Therefore it is said that victorious warriors win first and then go to war, while defeated warriors go to war first and then seek to win. (Cleary 1988, 20)

The commentator is referring to planning. Before ever entering into a conflict, the principal should have already devised a strategy. She does not want to "make it up" as she goes. Rather, actions should be deliberate and planned, so as to resolve the matter as quickly and in as least costly a manner as possible.

Another way to avoid conflict is to immediately give the adversary what he wants. In other words, would giving in be a deleterious approach, or would allowing the other satisfaction avoid a larger conflict without taking anything significant away from the principal in the first place? (Lin, 42). Again, there is a Buddhist saying which is similar in its meaning: give away the victory and take the defeat.

Imagine that, for the sake of convenience, you ask teachers to turn in their weekly reports stapled on the right side. If all reports come in this way, you will have an easier time organizing them. However, about 10 percent of the staff staples the papers on the left or dog-ears them, or simply hands them in in a loose pile. You have sent out memos on this issue three times.

Is this issue worth a fight? Do you have to get your way? In the end, does it matter? You could start writing letters of reprimand about insubordination to those refusing to comply with what you see as a reasonable administrative request. That would undoubtedly start a flurry of paper, grumbling, and grievance. Which is more important, that you get the reports in a timely manner or that teachers must comply with your format request in this situation?

Clearly, not getting your way on something so simple is frustrating, but is it worth pursuing? What will be the cost to morale and reputation if you do? Would it not be better to rise above the pettiness of the noncompliance, give those few teachers the victory in this case, and simply collect their reports? A power struggle here is simply not worth the effort.

Backing away, giving others the victory in this case, does not diminish your position and ensures that you get the information you need. A leader can descend into petty battles all too easily. Instead, a more productive response would be to forget one's ego and simply let go. The principal does not need the reputation as an obstinate, detail-demanding individual.

## THE PARKING LOT

There is random parking in the school lot. One teacher always parks in the same spot and considers it hers. She gets quite upset when someone is in the spot before she arrives, and she complains to the principal bitterly on these occasions. The principal has never wanted to get into the need to assign and police parking spaces. However, the disgruntled teacher has now enlisted several others who would like assigned spots.

A successful leader would quickly see that this battle would not be worth fighting. Conflict leaves winners and losers and can have the effect of making some people angry or bitter, feeling that they have not been adequately heard.

You could ignore the whole mess, but that would leave some teachers believing that you did not value their concerns. You could meet with them and present all the reasons why you do not want to spend energy on such a matter, but that could lead to endless discussion with your finally pulling rank.

What if you gave in by assigning random numbers corresponding to parking slots to teachers? This would not guarantee the original complainant her desired parking area, but it is a compromise which gets the job done and should satisfy the basic problem. Take the defeat and give away the victory.

It is easier, less costly, and more supportive to do so. In the end, the principal loses a bit of time but avoids what might become endless headaches over the matter. Because the principal does not engage in conflict, then no one can engage him (Lin 2006, 133).

What a simple concept. If you do not fight or compete, then no one can fight or compete with you. Leadership is not about getting your way or dominating others. It is about following others, getting out of the way, and nurturing the best in people.

## THE NONCOMPLIANT STUDENT

A student refuses to sit down in class. As long as he is not bothering anybody, let him stand. He will eventually get tired and sit down. In the meanwhile, the teacher (leader) has avoided a useless power struggle. She is not competing; she is not determined to have her way. Instead, she is allowing the natural flow of energy to take its course, without trying to control or interfere if she does not have to.

One enters battle (competition) only as a last resort. "Because she competes with no one, no one can compete with her" (Mitchell 1988, 66). How can you get into a fight if you refuse to engage in that way?

If a leader must fight, then she should do so with compassion for those involved.

Fighting with the intent to destroy the enemy or to expand the leader's ego will not lead to success. Here success means not just winning, but doing so in the least destructive and most compassionate manner (Lin, 135).

## DO NOT LOVE A GOOD FIGHT

Fighting with anger, pride, and relish will ultimately lead to resentment and the loss of loyalty within the staff. You do not want a reputation for enjoying fights. A principal should always remember that everyone in the fight is a human being, with all the strengths and frailties of humanity. She respects this. She avoids the Pyrrhic victory in order to save the larger good of the organization. Individual ego has no place here. You do not use a shotgun to kill a fly.

A teacher may insist that all students write with pens. If one student continues to persist in writing with a pencil, is it better to accept pencil instead of no paper at all? A teacher may not accept late work. In the end, though, is it better to have a late paper than no paper at all? There can always be some penalty for writing in pencil or finishing work late that is short of an absolute rejection.

All or nothing in these cases is hard to defend and can lead to significant conflict. Rigidity leads to snapping in two, while some flexibility allows for a more peaceful existence.

When one enters or avoids conflict in this way, she is in concert with the Tao. Consequently circumstances and supports will naturally arise out of the situation to help the leader. People will be more likely to comply if the request is not done in anger, but rather with kindness, respect, and neutrality.

There is an art to being noncontentious. Lao Tzu elaborates in chapter 68 of the *Tao Te Ching*:

> The great generals are not warlike
> The great warriors do not get angry
> Those who are good at defeating enemies do not engage them
> Those who are good at managing people lower themselves
> It is called the virtue of non-contention
> It is called the power of managing people
> It is called being harmonious with Heaven
> The ultimate principle of the ancients. (Lin 2006, 137)

What does it mean for a great general to be not warlike? Is the general not the head of an army, a group of warriors? Great leaders do not like or seek battle and conflict. They take no pleasure in the encounter. Their aim is to win the day without battle. They understand the price of battle.

Similarly, great warriors do not get angry. They do what they have to do, motivated by virtue and right action, not emotions. A leader has to keep his feelings in check so as not to lose control of himself or the situation. Anger leads to mistakes and unhappiness. When emotions are in control, then the leader is not. Feelings must be tempered by thoughtful action.

Above all, entering into conflict must be done deliberately for the good of all and not out of passion or the desire for gain. Here is what Sun Tzu has to say:

> A government should not mobilize an army out of anger, military leaders should not provoke war out of wrath. Act when it is beneficial, desist if it is not. Anger can revert to joy, wrath can revert to delight, but a nation destroyed

cannot be restored to existence, and the dead cannot be restored to life. Therefore an enlightened government is careful about this, a good military leadership is alert to this. This is the way to secure a nation and keep the armed forces whole. (Cleary 1988, 163)

Entering into battle or conflict is perilous. Although a principal does not conduct actual military maneuvers, the analogy is clear.

## IF YOU MUST FIGHT

First, Sun Tzu reminds us not to enter battle under the influence of anger, as seen by Lao Tzu as well. Then if you must engage, be very careful. Always make sure that you have planned for the peace after the battle. If a principal alienates staff or completely unbalances the staff in an effort to get what he wants, the school may be damaged permanently.

For instance, it would not be wise to create a new school-wide rule because of a single incident in a single classroom, no matter how annoyed it made you feel. Because one teacher speaks cruelly to a student, you do not give the entire faculty a compulsory script.

Ill feelings and anger can diminish in time. However, if relationships are destroyed, if people are completely alienated, then the damage is likely to be irreversible.

Imagine that there was a problem student in your school. He does not misbehave so much as have a problematic attitude. He is arrogant and aloof. He acts as if he has nothing to learn from his teacher. The teacher gets increasingly frustrated and annoyed by the student's manner. She takes it as a personal affront. Then, at the insistence of the student's mother, he is evaluated for learning disabilities. He does, indeed, qualify for special education, and the team develops an IEP for him.

The teacher is beside herself. She cannot believe that this student has managed to get legal protections that will force her to treat him with deference and accommodation. She cannot separate the situation from her feelings of aversion to this student. She sees this as the system letting her down. She not only does not get her way, but she is also cornered into an unacceptable (to her) position. She is ready for battle.

The principal tries on several occasions to explain calmly that the IEP is a legal document, that the team acted appropriately, and that there is really no option but to follow the accommodations. The teacher continues to see this as a win/lose situation. Eventually she forces the administrator to pull rank, entering fully into conflict with her.

This teacher and the principal had been very close colleagues when they were both teaching, and then for several more years after one had been promoted. Now that the principal could not avoid conflict, the results are anger, frustration, and bitterness. What is lost is the deep friendship that once was. The relationship is destroyed, a high price to pay for victory. Could this principal have avoided conflict, or was the situation developing into an inevitable confrontation?

Sun Tzu says:

> Even though opponents are numerous, they can be made not to fight. (Cleary 1988, 89)

Certainly, the opponent in this case is formidable. She is a well-established teacher, respected by parents and students alike, with a strong will and powerful emotions. The principal is not going to change her character, so what might he have done differently in this case?

Perhaps he could have made sure that the teacher was part of the evaluation team which determined the disability and IEP. She would then have been a full part of the process and expressed her feelings to the group. The IEP would not then have come as such a shock. Also, her anger might have been diverted to the team and the process, rather than toward the principal. Anger at a committee is different than anger at single person, and can dissipate in time.

## VICTORY WITHOUT ENGAGEMENT

You have experienced that teacher, student, or parent who knows just how to get to you, to push your buttons. If you give in to that anger, then you have lost control of yourself. You will probably do or say something that you will regret later. Here again, if the individual wants to say what she thinks will annoy you, let her. Give her the victory. The words will not hurt you unless you allow them to. Operate from a position of integrity, virtue, and neutrality.

How can you defeat your enemies without engaging them? The successful leader finds other means to disempower those who would oppose her. A department head had to gather teachers' thoughts on a particularly contentious curriculum matter. She knew she would have to deal with one teacher who was obstructionist, undermining, and antagonistic. He was going to commandeer the discussion for his own purposes.

To engage this teacher would simply lead to endless argument. The department head arrived at the meeting room early, and wrote this on the board. "Write your ideas about XX and put them in the folder on the desk." In this way, everyone had a chance to express him or herself, but the problem teacher was disarmed. There would be no debate at this time, no confrontation. The department head had avoided conflict and still managed to collect the information she had sought.

The wise principal will follow this advice from Sun Tzu:

> Therefore those who win every battle are not really skillful—those who render others' armies helpless without fighting are the best of all. (Cleary 1988, 34)

Winning every battle is not necessarily a sign of skillful leadership. One can wield power with no other purpose than to get one's way. This style will eventually lead to diminished power, dissatisfaction, and possibly rebellion. How do you render others' armies helpless? Applied to schools, this may sound harsh. However, the basic concept is to avoid battle entirely.

That is exactly what the illustration above describes. By taking away the teacher's opportunity to be argumentative and disruptive without taking away his right to express his opinion, the leader has rendered him (the other's army) helpless. There is no battle, yet the supervisor gets the information he needs.

Other ways to render the enemy "helpless" might be to build a position or argument which takes in his needs. If the argument is sound enough, without any logical holes, then it may actually be unassailable. Once again, there is no point for the opponent to attack. There is no battle. As long as the principal keeps herself on the moral high ground, this technique can be helpful.

## PLANNING

As Sun Tzu says:

> Those who use arms well cultivate the Way and keep the rules. Thus they can govern in such a way as to prevail over the corrupt. (Cleary 1988, 64)

At all times, a crucial aspect of avoiding battle is planning. The examples in this chapter show how the skillful leader works with a situation rather than confronts it with mere force. A good principal knows his people, the topic, the forces at work, and only then does he act, if he chooses to act at all. In the parking example above, the principal avoids confrontation through planning before significant conflict arises.

> Therefore a victorious army first wins and then seeks battle; a defeated army first battles and then seeks victory. (Cleary 1988, 64)

By planning first, the leader assures victory. In other words, she does not enter into the conflict before she has a plan which she knows will be successful. To start fighting and hope everything comes out all right is a dangerous strategy. Once again, the supervisor of the argumentative teacher plans before the confrontation occurs. The principal in the parking example offers a solution before there is any real confrontation. This minimizes that conflict and leads to a "victory" for the leader.

## THE HUMBLE LEADER

Returning to chapter 68 of the *Tao Te Ching* cited above, we ask how a leader manages people by lowering himself. Arrogance begets anger and resentment. Humility allows one to lead without offending others. A great leader does not work by fiat. Instead, he realizes that others may have ideas or understanding better than his, given a particular subject.

If a principal wants to improve classroom behaviors, then he would be prudent to ask teachers for suggestions. After all, the principal is no longer in the classroom, so his ideas would not be seen as relevant as those of classroom teachers who have immediate experience in the situation.

By using the natural energies and information around him, along with humility and neutrality, the effective leader solves problems and can work with difficult situations. There can be no arrogance, nothing dictatorial, no anger. At times, problems will work themselves out if the principal can resist tampering with the situation. The resolution may not even be what the leader would have seen as the best arrangement, but if it worked and the staff was content, then so be it.

Mitchell concludes the verse in his translation this way, showing the light touch of the leader:

> All of them embody
> the virtue of non-competition.
> Not that they don't like to compete,
> but they do it in the spirit of play.
> In this they are like children
> and in harmony with the Tao. (Mitchell 1988, 68)

The principal is transparent and as innocent as a child. There are no hidden motives. There is no strong negative or positive emotion. There is only flowing with what is happening, allowing the Tao to lead her as she leads the staff.

A common image is that of the yielding reed and broken oak, suggesting that bending and yielding are more likely characteristics of survival than standing rigid in a storm. This idea was also known to Lao Tzu (Lin, 153).

Confrontation without the ability to yield or adapt is a precursor to self-destruction. The successful leader knows when to back away, give in to others, and live to fight another day.

Trying to force your ideas or orders onto others may work in the short run, but eventually it will erode any base of support and alienate the staff. Perhaps a principal can force teachers to teach with doors open or doors closed, but is this worth the hassle? You can show and assert your power for a time, but the price is high.

You will eventually break yourself against the staff, who will resent and resist you. An autocratic style seldom works in schools. A principal can get much more done through support, compromise, and thoughtful action, which not only garners compliance but also loyalty and acceptance.

This is why gentle leaders are successful. Such leaders may appear soft or weak, but in fact they are in a superior position to those who are powerful and bold. We see this theme of humility in leadership throughout the *Tao Te Ching*. Those who bluster, make lots of noise, and extol themselves inevitably fall, while those who are already on the ground, keeping to a low position, are the ones who are successful. Listen to and respect the staff.

Mitchell concludes the verse by making the point clearly and directly:

> The hard and stiff will be broken
> The soft and supple will prevail. (Mitchell 1988, 76)

## CASE STUDY 1

*You are one of two elementary school principals in your town. Because of population changes, each school now has about seventy-five students. Financially, combining the schools into one makes good sense. Taxes are on the rise. You know that such a consolidation will result in loss of staff, administrators, and support staff.*

*Because the two schools represent two parts of town, each has many loyal supporters who see the particular school as theirs. They went to that school, and now their children go to that school. Many of the teachers have taught both generations. Local civic events happen in these schools. Consequently, many people oppose closing one of the schools, even though these same people complain about the rising tax burden in the town.*

*The school board wants your input. You are a principal, so you should have an informed decision about this matter. In fact, your spouse is a teacher at the school where you do not work. Many teachers in both schools are your personal friends. Your own children have attended elementary school in the town.*

*Teachers oppose the consolidation, as does the union. Nobody wants to see jobs lost. You are certainly in an emotional quandary. What are you going to say about all this? Where are your loyalties? What is the right thing to do?*

*No matter what you say, there will be those who agree with you and those who oppose your ideas. In fact, some of the opposition may be quite strident, because this issue has become an incendiary one in town. No matter what you say, you risk losing support, authority, and even your position. Board members are divided on what to do, so your input is of particular interest and will be examined closely.*

*A battle is surely coming. You receive phone calls every day, for and against the merger. You do not yet know what the other elementary school principal thinks, and you have not yet spoken to the superintendent on this matter. Members of your particular school's community have insisted that you hold forums, including parents, teachers, union officials, and other community members. The newspaper is anxious to hear what you have to say.*

1. Which lessons from this chapter could you apply to this situation?
2. How will you formulate your ultimate thinking on this issue?
3. How will you deal with your personal issues (loyalties, friendships, spouse's job, guilt over your decision, your own position)?
4. What are the natural forces and energies in this scenario?
5. Can you predict the outcomes that might occur depending on what you have to say?
6. Where will you turn for advice?
7. Is there any way to avoid this confrontation?
8. Is there a strategy which will allow you to win without a fight or ill feelings?
9. Should you and the other principal offer a joint statement?
10. If you must enter the fray, how will you do so? What will be your strategy?

## CASE STUDY 2

*Ms. Jones is a second-year teacher, both years having been in your school. She is unhappy with the schedule and wants something done about it. She sees you, the principal, as the person with the authority to answer her complaints and make the school a better place for her.*

*Among her complaints are the following:*

1. She does not have enough preparation time.

2. She has too many students to be effective.
3. She does not like cafeteria duty and would like a different assignment.
4. She wants a longer lunch break.
5. School ends too late in the afternoon for her to get to her yoga class.

*Ms. Jones is an excellent teacher, one of the best you have seen despite her lack of experience. You know that you will want her on your side in the future, and you hope that she will continue to work at your school. She would be difficult to replace. The kids like her, as does the staff. She gets along well with parents and is generally active in the community.*

*She has been talking to union officials and other teachers. Several very fine teachers are backing her in her pursuit of change. You are receiving phone calls from parents who like and support her. One of these is the chair of the school board. Your superintendent has gotten wind of this potential issue and has asked you to deal with it.*

*With all this going on, you cannot afford to make enemies. You have to find a delicate balance which will allow you to deal with the situation without alienating allies or good teachers or the board. Can it be done?*

1. Whicht lessons from this chapter can you apply to the situation?
2. What are the natural forces and energies in this situation?
3. Is there a way to avoid the confrontation with Ms. Jones?
4. Is this going to end up in a power struggle?
5. Are all of her grievances reasonable?
6. How can you bring her into the solution?
7. Is this a battle you have to fight?
8. What will your ultimate strategy be?

*Chapter Five*

# Paradoxes of Leadership

### EAST VS. WEST

While Lao Tzu might not have been aware of the West, he was aware of people who believed in the same types of values as many of those in the West. For this reason, much of his wisdom appears paradoxical as we read it. Many of the ideas we take for granted are specifically held up for scrutiny, and appear to be the opposite of what is advantageous. Consequently, Taoism presents many paradoxes for the Western mind.

Chapter 19 of the *Tao Te Ching* begins:

> Banish the intellectual!
> Discard knowledge!
> We will all benefit a hundredfold! (Dale 2002, 39)

Wisdom and knowledge are essential, but unless they are converted into action, they offer little benefit. Imagine all of those theories we teach in courses to prepare educational administrators. Has any principal not experienced the difficulty of trying to do what appears so natural in print? Try building consensus, for instance. Knowing is not enough. Even knowing how is not enough. Knowing what to do or not to do is crucial.

Sun Tzu brings up an interesting paradox of knowing. He tells us:

> Therefore, those who are not thoroughly aware of the disadvantages in the use of arms cannot be thoroughly aware of the advantages in the use of arms. (Cleary 1988, 23)

In other words, to know something one must also know its opposite, or other side. An individual defines peace in terms of war, plenty in terms of want, and so on. This kind of knowledge allows the leader to choose action wisely.

Providing everyone with everything he or she wants is a form of plenty. However, this can create a belief that people can have even more, and spoiled individuals feel a new level of want.

Actually applying knowledge effectively is what makes effectiveness. Knowing the most does not make a principal the most effective leader. Experience as well as book learning are necessary for success. There is never a one-to-one correspondence between one's academic learning and one's abilities in the job.

## NAMING

By defining concepts, we invite their opposites as well. For instance, once we define benevolence, we have also defined the lack of benevolence, or ill will. Naming a concept would seem to be gaining understanding of that concept, but actually the opposite may occur. By naming, we limit the meaning rather than seeing the idea in a purely objective light.

> End benevolence, abandon righteousness
> The people return to piety and charity (Lin 2006, 39)

Once you have defined benevolence and ill will, you have limited your scope of understanding of individuals' actions. For instance, if benevolence is generosity and good nature, does an impoverished person's failure to contribute to a good cause serve as an example of ill will or selfishness? Does a cancer patient's contribution to cancer research constitute benevolence or self-interest? Labeling prevents our thinking more deeply about the actions themselves, instead of quickly putting them into prefabricated boxes.

Imagine that a teacher has sent a student to your office for a dress-code violation. You see the student's clothing is, indeed, in noncompliance. Dress-code violation = counterculture kid = troublemaker = problem = penalty. Everything is neatly explained. However, if you look at the student and not just the violation, actually try to find out what is going on, you may be surprised.

Perhaps the student honestly does not know the policy. The student may be of poverty, and these are the only clothes he has to wear. Maybe the child is living on the street. What would you do if you found out that the student was transgendered, and that that was the cause of the unusual clothing? In each case, your response would likely not be a lock-step application of the dress code.

We would consider naming concepts a form of knowledge. Knowledge is good and powerful stuff. Understanding the policy is also a positive attribute of the leader. Taken together, this principal knows what the policy handbook says to do and does it. However, if he looked at the student's actions as just that, without automatically characterizing them according to definition, he might find out a host of information which would then inform what he does in this situation.

## PARADOXES IN ACTION

In chapter 22 of the *Tao Te Ching,* Lao Tzu writes:

> To be ready for wholeness, first be fragmented.
> To be ready for rightness, first be wronged.
> To be ready for fullness, first be empty.
> To be ready for renewal, first be worn out.
> To be ready for success, first fail.
> To be ready for doubt, first be certain. (Dale 2002, 45)

This series of paradoxes points to major themes of Taoism. To truly comprehend a condition, the leader has to have experienced both the condition and its opposite. The two polar positions define each other.

By experiencing being fragmented, the leader understands wholeness. She understands the value of fragmentation as well as the value of wholeness. Is it not better to yield (fragmented/soft) than to become too whole, too committed before being sure of the situation? Yielding to the interests of others can be a sign of her allowing herself to be "wronged," while at the same time being right, as we have seen several times already.

To be empty is to allow for fullness by not committing too soon to one course of action. Emptiness is total potential, infinite possibility. A leader cannot renew herself without first having expended the effort to be worn out.

Experiencing failure and uncertainty allows the leader to understand success and certainty. Again, reaching for success too early, or believing in certainty too early are recipes for trouble.

To be low is to be humble. In that position, a leader can garner the trust and good will of the staff. If a principal enters a situation with the attitude that she already knows everything, then she will alienate others. She will miss the knowledge and experience others have to offer by refusing to listen. She may be right, but her methods have cost her much.

This entire passage is about humility in leadership. Where we might imagine a bold display, the Tao tells us that effective leaders keep themselves humble. By being just the opposite of powerful and imposing, they receive what they need, including the support of their people.

# HUMILITY

The Lin translation of the chapter continues:

> Therefore the sages hold to the one as an example for the world
> Without flaunting themselves—and so are seen clearly
> Without presuming themselves—and so are distinguished
> Without praising themselves—and so have merit
> Without boasting about themselves—and so are lasting. (Lin 2006, 45)

The paradoxes here are particularly interesting and hit at the heart of much of the Western approach to life. Flaunting, presuming, praising, and boasting are all vehicles for making a person stand out, appearing to be exceptional. However, Lao Tzu tells us that just the opposite is true. A person who does not perform these actions is, in fact, one who stands out, one who is distinguished, one who has merit, and one who lasts.

For the educational leader, this means to stand out by virtue of being humble. It is okay not to have all the answers. A principal can defer to the ideas of others without shame. She does not have to involve herself in every situation or even solve every problem. A leader can follow as well as lead, depending on what the circumstances call for.

# "SUBTLE PERCEPTION"

Chapter 36 of the *Tao Te Ching* offers more paradoxical advice:

> If you want to shrink something,
> you must first allow it to expand.
> If you want to get rid of something,
> you must first allow it to flourish.
> If you want to take something,
> you must first allow it to be given.
> This is called the subtle perception
> of the way things are. (Mitchell 1988, 36)

The only way to shrink something is first to make it big. Think of a balloon. You cannot shrink it until you first blow it up. A leader may proudly blow himself up, but this only invites attacks by those he ignores or lords over. Eventually, they will shrink him down to size.

Similarly, by building up one's worth, one appears to be strengthened, to flourish. However, exaggerated self-aggrandizement will eventually be exposed. Then the leader will be wearing the emperor's new clothes. People will see through the false buildup, the transparent front. They will get rid of his ego for him.

A thing cannot be taken before it is owned or accepted. In other words, if you promote something too much (such as your particular system of discipline) with no exceptions, others will eventually get tired of it. They will want their say, some control.

As you continue to advertise, persuade, enforce, presume, and demand your point of view, others will become increasingly alienated. Eventually, the leader will have to discard the idea in the face of the need for others to be heard. Giving too much of your own point of view takes away, or disempowers, the perceptions of others.

Finally, the idea of giving to receive is well known. If you want to make money, then you have to invest money. If you want to be treated with respect, then you must respect others. This is just common sense.

As do the other paradoxes, these apparent contradictions refer to humility. They show that shrinking, weakening, discarding, seizing are all realized through their opposite actions. That is why these ideas can be referred to as "subtle clarity." The obvious paths and answers are not necessarily the way to go. A successful leader has to think at more subtle levels.

## THE LUNCH MENU

Perhaps students are complaining about the lunch menu. They do not like the more nutritious foods and want more pizza, hamburgers, and french fries. You need to shrink their desire for "junk" food. You decide to offer only salad and grilled cheese as nutritious choices.

For main courses you offer only chicken nuggets. After a month of this, the students are so tired of this new menu that they welcome more choices, even if they are foods that are good for them. You give in to their wishes to the point where those wishes become less dominating.

## SOFT AND HARD

Chapter 43 of the *Tao Te Ching* begins with these lines:

> The most soft and ethereal things of the world
> Will always penetrate the hard and unyielding. (Bright-Fey 2006, 226)

What is soft and overrides that which is hard? Water can wear away at rock until there is the Grand Canyon. The wind and rain can wear mountains into nothing. Words can defeat an enemy at times better than weapons. Because something is hard does not make it invincible. In fact, the truth is just the opposite. Patience is everything.

Previous chapters have shown how soft methods, such as preparing the ground, building strategies, and even doing nothing can accomplish more than fighting or yelling might. Building an unassailable argument is better than having a shouting match. Strength of position can defeat strength of arms. We are often too eager to jump into a situation and do battle. This is not always necessary.

As a side note, the Mitchell translation uses the word "overcomes" instead of "overrides" (Mitchell 1988, 43). This word choice has a sense of strength and power. To overcome something is to put it in its place, not to let it defeat you. We overcome our fears, our faults, and our opponents.

## "ACT WITHOUT ACTION"

> How can a leader do the following?
> Act without action
> Manage without meddling (Lin 2006, 127)

Earlier chapters have examined the idea of action and nonaction. A successful leader must carefully choose his actions and timing. To act without acting is to do what is right without trying to control events. Working with the Tao, or the natural energy patterns of a situation, is to work with it, not against it.

This is also acting without meddling. The principal does not try to tamper with what is going on to make everything just the way he wants it. Perhaps he prefers a trimester system to a quarter system, but the school has had a tradition of quarters for decades. Does he want to meddle with what is working because of his own preferences, or is it best left alone? There is no reason to pick away at processes and systems which are working adequately just to suit his own biases.

Lao Tzu explains how to prepare for action. The effective leader will break down complex situations into smaller bits, such as dividing up a process into its individual steps. This is why, he says, a leader should never attempt a huge enterprise, but approach it through its smaller parts and thus find success (Lin, 127).

The complex is accomplished through the simple, the large through the small. If a leader breaks up the large and complex tasks into smaller pieces, then she can more easily handle what is going on.

Zhang Yu, who wrote commentary on *The Art of War* during the Sung Dynasty, appreciates the paradox of planning, that a winning army assures its victory not by battle but by planning. In other words, the battle is over before it begins.

Therefore it is said that victorious warriors win first and then go to war, while defeated warriors go to war first and then seek to win. (Cleary 1988, 20)

## THE NEW BLOCK SCHEDULE

A principal and a committee of teachers decide that they want to convert a seven-period day to a four-block day. This shift is both complex and enormous. However, the task can be subdivided.

Try a few volunteer courses at first and see what can be learned. Then amass information illustrating the advantages and disadvantages of the block format. Share this with staff and the board. Explain the proposed change to the parents. Send groups of staff, board members, and community members to observe schools which run the block format.

Provide inservice workshops for teachers offering techniques for the long block, so that they understand how to make the entire time meaningful and interesting for students. Have discussions around the conflict between broader coverage and deeper coverage. At the same time, you might add some more volunteer courses to the block ones.

Finally, you are ready to make the huge change to the block schedule. However, it seems like a small step, since you have already taken so many smaller steps on your way toward that end. The sage leader does not attempt great deeds, and achieves greatness because of it. Imagine the chaos if the principal had simply declared the change to block scheduling.

## HUMILITY EQUALS POWER

One of the significant ideas of the Tao is that the leader needs to be humble to be powerful.

> Why do all the hundreds of great rivers
> Flow naturally to the sea?
> because the sea is always lower than the rivers.
> When are thousands of people attracted to a sage?
> When she positions herself below them,
> always listening, tirelessly responding to their needs. (Dale 2002, 133)

Water always seeks the lowest level, yet, as mentioned earlier, water can carve out the Grand Canyon.

People would rather follow a humble leader than one who constantly boasts, comparing himself advantageously to others. By staying low, the successful leader shows himself not as a powermonger but as a simple, respectful soul. The humble listen to others, serve them, and fulfill their needs.

If the principal shows humility, she is in a position to garner loyalty and support. By not putting herself above the staff, she shows that she is one of the staff, not separate from them.

Leading from behind, the principal can support the staff, following their direction. Leading from behind, the principal gains the respect and trust of the staff. Rather than pulling people in a direction that they do not understand or agree with, working with natural energies and inclinations may be a more successful path to take (Lin 2006, 133).

Everyone knows the leader who must have his way. He dismisses the ideas of others and drags the institution kicking and screaming in his chosen direction. The example of moving to a block schedule above illustrates a more gentle and supportive style for moving the institution. Working with as opposed to doing to is the way to move a group. Do not try to appear omniscient and omnipotent. Do not fear to ask the question to which you do not know the answer.

## THE THREE TREASURES

Lao Tzu continues to offer apparent paradoxes to his readers:

> I have three treasures
> I hold to them and protect them
> The first is called compassion
> The second is called conservation
> The third is called not daring to be ahead in the world
> Compassionate, thus able to have courage
> Conserving, thus able to reach widely
> Not daring to be ahead in the world
> Thus able to assume leadership
> Now if one has courage but discards compassion
> Reaches widely but discards conservation
> Goes ahead but discards being behind
> Then death! (Lin 2006, 135)

This book has discussed the humility of the leader extensively. This is why one does not dare to be ahead in the world. One does not often think of compassion as necessary for courage. Courage needs compassion in several ways.

First, a leader has to be compassionate toward something, an idea, a cause, a project, in order to display courage. How can a leader be courageous with respect to something she cares little about?

Second, if the leader is dealing with opponents, then she needs to show them compassion. Yes, the principal wants to win, but not at the cost of the good will and good works of the "enemy." Do not drive people away with your powerful courage. Instead, keep them on your side for another day by using compassionate courage, embracing them even as you argue with them.

Conserving refers to avoiding waste. If a leader spreads his assets too thinly, then he will be weak. If he wastes too much while trying to spread the area of his influence, he will be in danger. The successful leader, as seen above, does not lay waste to his opponents. He does not win at the cost of having disgruntled, disloyal, and even angry people to work with.

## SUBTLE ACTIONS

Lao Tzu continues to explain that

> The Tao of Heaven:
> Does not contend and yet excels in winning
> Does not speak and yet excels in responding
> Is not summoned and yet comes on its own
> Is unhurried and yet excels in planning
> The heavenly net is vast
> Loose, and yet does not let anything slip through. (Lin 2006, 147)

This passage cuts to the core of Taoist leadership, again presenting the concepts in apparent paradoxes, such as not contending and yet winning. As we have seen, contentiousness is not necessary for success.

Knowing what is happening, understanding who and what you are dealing with, planning, and careful consideration of actions all combine to help a leader succeed without conflict. Conflict inevitably leads to bad ends; at the very least, alienation of some of the staff or other members of the educational community.

How can a leader respond without speaking? A good principal does what needs to be done without having to speak about it. He can spend hours explaining and debating and announcing, or he can simply do. The good leader should note trouble spots without being told where they are. He should sense discontent or frustration. Once these conditions are known to him, he acts on them to right the situation.

Talking about what you are going to do is much easier than doing it. We all know those who talk a good game but then fail to follow through, resulting in distrust and eventual lack of support.

The successful leader is not hurried. She does not run around flapping her arms, planning for everything in a panic. She takes her time, planning carefully and deliberately out of a state of calm concentration. She does not reach conclusions until after she has studied the situation and completed her analysis. Then in a planful way she can respond to a situation, ready to act intelligently and successfully.

The successful principal remains calm and deliberate, as relaxed as possible, while dealing with the day-to-day challenges of the job. Like the Tao, he is easygoing, vast and loose, but he does not miss anything. The leader must be laid back and vigilant at the same time, watching carefully but not being reactive. He has a solid sense of self and position, and a trust in his ability to do what needs to be done. He is a steady influence and a good shepherd.

## FLEXIBILITY, NOT RIGIDITY

To win the day, flexibility, not rigidity, is necessary. A good leader knows when to yield, and thus retain her power. To bend is to be strong (Lin, 153). This is not unlike the contemporary expression that the reed bends in the wind, but the mighty oak remains straight. However, if the wind becomes strong enough, the oak will break while the reed continues to bend.

We tend to associate standing one's ground with strength. To a point, as with the oak, this makes sense. However, what appears as strength can become obstinacy and rigid behavior, a refusal to either admit defeat or being wrong. This is not ultimately productive, as it breeds anger, fear, disloyalty, and lack of trust. Strength resides in flexibility, not an unmoving position. It is good to know when to yield in order to fight another day.

If there are good points in the opponent's position, then incorporate them into your own. Do not stand stubbornly refusing to move or accommodate. You may get your way, but this will be only a temporary victory. Winning through intimidation, fear, and obstinance will eventually turn against you.

Return to the example of moving from a conventional to a block schedule. If the principal did this by fiat, he might get his way, but there would be anger, resentment, and vengefulness within the staff.

How much more productive and lasting the change would be if the leader incorporated teacher ideas, provided strong inservice, made the change gradually, put staff members in charge of various aspects of the process. By being "soft" one can gain what being "hard" will not obtain. Hard only appears to be tough, and soft only appears to be weak.

## THE CENTRAL PARADOX

These paradoxes of leadership, particularly those having to do with the appearance of strength and weakness, are at the heart of the Tao. The message continues to return, again and again, to humility, a soft-looking approach which wins in the end. Lack of humility is arrogance and egocentricity. It is telling others what to do, and putting your ideas first.

Lack of humility breeds alienation and resentment. Teachers will eventually stop voicing opinions or offering creative solutions as they give in to the atmosphere of powerlessness that the principal has created. Group morale will suffer, and good teachers may begin to look for more supportive places to work.

On the other hand, the principal may be in a position to know what ideas will work best. The problem then becomes making sure that teachers are heard, that the leader has clearly explained his position, and that he has kept alienation of the staff to a minimum. This is dangerous territory, and the principal must approach it accordingly, thinking through the possible options for action.

## CASE STUDY 1

*Teachers from grades 3, 4, and 5 come to you with a proposal for Women's History Month. These teachers, both men and women, are passionate about this project, citing the dearth of women celebrated in the social studies series the school uses.*

*You, the principal, have always had mixed feelings about this sort of thing. Doesn't such an event further marginalize women by separating them from "regular" history, as if they are a separate topic? Why not include more women in the standard curriculum?*

*What you want to do is change the books that the school uses for social studies. You would like teachers to search out better texts with regard to the inclusion of minorities. This would have several advantages. First, no one would have to arrange any special units outside the text. Then, celebrating individual groups' contributions to history would truly be a celebration and not a segregation of various groups of people.*

*Nevertheless, teachers have researched their ideas well and present you with a quality proposal, something truly worthy of these fine teachers. Your quandary is whether to go along with their ideas and go for what you see as a short-term solution, or hold on to your major goal of revising the curriculum in general. This will take considerably longer to do than will the proposal before you.*

*There are also risks involved. Even though you see your ideas as the best solution in terms of the curriculum, a large part of the community has been complaining about the lack of diversity in the social studies program. Some powerful individuals, including members of the local historical society, have been after the school to make changes for several years. Your idea may be seen as a refusal to diversify, and the teachers have offered a sound educational plan.*

*There is also the risk of alienating the staff. Since they have come up with an excellent piece of curriculum work, how would they feel if their time, energy, and ideas were rejected for your broader vision, even if you explained your arguments well? You could always form a committee in response to their proposal and use it as a means of getting across what you would like to see.*

*Clearly you have a dilemma on your hands. Do you do what you think is educationally the best thing, do you accept or reject the teachers' work, do you try to explain your position to the interested community members? Will the creation of a committee be very disappointing, and appear as a smoke screen for your cause? What are you going to do?*

1. Whicht ideas from this chapter can you apply to this case?
2. Will the teachers' proposal derail or just postpone the implementation of your ideas?
3. Are you sure your vision is better than the teachers'?
4. Who will you have to answer to regardless of which way you choose to go?
5. What are the chances that you will seriously alienate some of the faculty if you hold your ground?
6. Which issues of leadership should you consider?
7. Is there a plan which would satisfy everyone?
8. What are you going to do?

## CASE STUDY 2

*Students and teachers alike want flavored waters in the vending machines. The school has been moving in the direction of providing healthier food and snacks. There is no longer any soda for sale. Snacks like candy and potato chips are no longer in the vending machines or part of school lunch.*

*You, the principal, have researched the various brands of flavored water and found them to be more or less nutritionally neutral. Still, you feel that allowing these waters will set a bad precedent. They will become the gateway to more and more low nutrition foods and drinks.*

*Paradoxes of Leadership* 69

*You decide to stand your ground on this issue. Students have presented a well-done petition with hundreds of signatures. In faculty meetings, teachers have voiced their support of the students and their cause. However, you have already made your decision. You have checked around, and no other school sells these drinks.*

*The climate is getting tense. Many students are bringing flavored water from home to drink during lunch or free time. They are openly protesting your position, but within school rules. Several clubs start selling flavored water at sports events as fund-raisers. Teachers buy the product on these occasions.*

*Finally, one of the cafeteria juice vending machines is vandalized. Someone has written all over the front such phrases as, "MS is a control freak" and "All we ask is freedom to choose our own foods." This is making you increasingly uncomfortable.*

*You have a dilemma. The opposition is getting very large. However, you have hung your hat on this issue, making a big deal out of your refusal to allow flavored drinks to be sold. Then you deliberately stuck to your decision to demonstrate resolve as part of your leadership. To reverse yourself now would make you look foolish and defeated, a flip-flopper. You have been accused by some of being weak and backing down from issues. This seemed to be the perfect opportunity to counter that accusation.*

*Individuals are beginning to talk to school board members. There are editorials about this issue in the local paper and the school paper. One day, almost all of the students wear black and drink nothing during school hours. They boycott the vending machines in the cafeteria. What a mess.*

1. Which lessons from this chapter can you apply to the situation?
2. As a leader, it is important to stick by your guns. How does that apply here?
3. What will happen the next time students petition for a change at the school?
4. What was the price of your holding your ground?
5. How might you have handled the situation differently?
6. Can you find any common ground here?
7. What reputation will you have as a result of this incident?
8. What will you do at the point where students are protesting in the school?

*Chapter Six*

# Themes and Images

There are numerous other themes and images in Taoism which could inform educational leadership. This chapter will examine some of these ideas.

## FLEXIBILITY

A key theme of the *Tao Te Ching* is flexibility. The movement of the Tao is cyclical. The myriad things of the universe arise from it and return to it. Nothing is permanent (Lin, 81). Everything is in a state of flux. To be successful, a leader must understand this and be ready to let go of specific beliefs and points of view as situations change. A principal who wants to run his school as if he lived in the 1950s will not be able to confront the challenges of the twenty-first century.

Themes and ideas of the past may no longer hold true. Old assumptions may no longer apply. There was a time when students were worried about being sent to the office because they were in trouble. There was a time when parents backed up the school in issues of discipline. Now, students can be defiant. Many parents immediately take the side of their children and fight with the school over issues of discipline and punishment. The world changes, and successful people change with it.

According to Derek Lin, "weak" can mean pliant and flexible, as is the case with living beings (Lin, 80). The Tao is a life force. Living things are supple and pliant. The dead are stiff and dry. To be part of the living, part of the Tao, one then must be willing to bend and grow, to be flexible and adaptable. As we have seen in *The Art of War*, a successful leader changes tactics with the circumstances and situation.

Lao Tzu tells us that the minds of leaders are constantly changing (Lin, 99). Their minds are flexible, always changing to adapt to new information, ideas, and situations. To stand still is to become rigid. To live and lead successfully is to be part of a constantly changing world.

Avoiding change does not work. Change is inevitable. So, to continue on means to be part of the ever-flowing river of life. Imagine trying to oppose the introduction of new communication and computing technologies in a school. The students and staff would be left far behind the rest of the world.

Sun Tzu was well-aware of the need for flexibility.

> Therefore victory in war is not repetitious, but adapts its form endlessly. (Cleary 1988, 93)

No two situations are the same. The principal must approach each issue separately, as something new. Victories are not repetitious; they are unique each time. Once again, this results in the need for constant adaptability.

Each situation is new and different. Simply because a strategy worked in the past, in a situation similar to the present one, does not mean that it will work again. Even subtle differences in conditions can result in the need for an entirely new approach. The principal may be dealing with people of a different culture or socioeconomic level or different educational level than those of the people the last time a similar incident occurred.

In *The Art of War*, Sun Tzu uses the image of water to elaborate on the need to be adaptive.

> So a military force has no constant formation, water has no constant shape: the ability to gain victory by changing and adapting to the opponent is called genius. (Cleary 1988, 94)

The principal, like the general, gains success by adapting to the situation. In the same way, water always takes on the shape of its container or of the terrain on which it flows.

As a situation unfolds, the principal is constantly moving, reading the signs, so she can adapt her strategy to what is happening. For instance, a leader would not use a directive style with well-established and experienced teachers unless absolutely necessary. At the same time, direction may be exactly what the new teacher needs as he finds his way.

Finally, Sun Tzu has this to say:

> Therefore generals who know all possible adaptations to take advantage of the ground know how to use military forces. If generals do not know how to adapt advantageously, even if they know the lay of the land they cannot take advantage of it. (Cleary 1988, 111)

## BE LIKE WATER

Water is used throughout the *Tao Te Ching* to express several other aspects of the Tao.

> The supreme good is like water,
> which nourishes all things without trying to.
> It is content with the low places people disdain.
> Thus it is like the Tao. (Mitchell 1988, 8)

Despite the highest goodness, water occupies the lowest position.

It always flows down and fills whatever shape contains it. Water resembles humility and adaptability. It assumes whatever shape is most practical and least disruptive to the environment.

Water benefits every living thing. It does not play favorites, and it does not fight. It simply follows its natural path, nurturing life along the way. Water is not afraid to occupy those places that others shun. By being humble and eschewing the grandiose, it stays on its simple course. Water does not grandstand.

A good leader is like this image of water. She nurtures everyone while remaining humble. The successful leader does not look for fame, and she is willing to do the tough work necessary to make the system work well. She accepts the simple tasks of nurturing and supporting, rather than telling and ordering. The good principal is with her people, not on top of them.

Lao Tzu also tells us that

> Nothing in the world is softer or weaker than water
> Yet nothing is better at overcoming the hard and strong
> This is because nothing can replace it. (Lin 2006, 157)

Water is infinitely adaptable. The principal must also be able to adapt to many situations. Sometimes he must be stern, sometimes lenient, and sometimes playful.

At the same time that water is so flexible and "weak," water can erode the hardest surface. Whole rocks give way to its power. The successful leader, like water, will be patient. She will also keep to the natural path, the flow of events, without too much meddling. She can appear weak but be tenacious at the same time.

Water gives life. Nothing can replace it. Good leadership gives life to an institution. As the principal follows the natural energies of a situation, she can see that oftentimes the situation can work itself out without interfering. By allowing events to take place, the principal may appear weak, but in fact he may be resisting the urge to tamper with what will eventually evolve naturally into a successful situation.

Sun Tzu may not mention water explicitly, but the lines below certainly bring it to mind.

> To advance irresistibly, push through their gaps. To retreat elusively, outspeed them. (Cleary 1988, 82)

The image of pushing through the gaps suggests the fluidity and adaptability of water. Water always finds the lowest and simplest path, thus at times keeping out of sight while rushing through ravines and rivers.

Perhaps you, the principal, are doing an observation of a teacher. You see that the fundamentals of being a good teacher are there, but they are not as yet well developed. You can approach the teacher in several ways. What happens if you choose the way of water?

First, the principal does not immediately place himself in a position superior to the teacher. He is already there by position, so there is no need to emphasize this. Rather, the principal will put himself in a nurturing position, beginning by honestly praising what the teacher did well.

Then, rather than telling the teacher what she did wrong, the principal asks her what she thought went well and what might need improvement. This is followed by gently questioning. For instance, "How might you improve student attention, especially in the back of the room?" The principal does not simply tell the teacher what to do, as would an arrogant superior. He allows her to find her own answers. By skillfully questioning her, the principal can eventually elicit a plan from the teacher.

In this case, the teacher has largely come up with her own critique and remedial plan. All the time, however, the principal is controlling the conversation subtly through his questions. By the end of the session, the teacher can say that she made the plan herself, through her own perceptions and insight.

The principal is content to play a secondary, supporting role. That is being like water. He willingly takes the lower position while giving full support to the teacher, allowing her to examine her own work. He does not come off as the person with the one and only set of answers and recommendations.

## KNOW YOURSELF

*The Art of War* explains the value of knowing oneself before acting:

> So it is said that if you know others and know yourself, you will not be imperiled in a hundred battles; if you do not know others but know yourself, you win one and lose one; if you do not know others and do not know yourself, you will be imperiled in every single battle. (Cleary 1988, 53)

The only way to be successful at all is to know who you are and what you are about. The leader has to be clear about his opinions and ideas. He needs to know his resources. He should be fully aware of his talents.

If the goal is to be successful every time you confront a situation, then knowing the self is necessary but not sufficient. The principal must know the enemy as well. Trying to do something without knowing what you are up against will likely result in failure. The principal needs to have her ducks in a row before confronting the board, angry parents, faculty, or students.

Sun Tzu also tells us to be respectful of the enemy.

> A surrounded army must be given a way out. (Cleary 1988, 108)

As seen in other chapters, crushing or humiliating your opponent may feel good temporarily, but the ultimate results will be a continued rift. Allow people to retain their pride and self-respect. The leader will likely want these individuals for another issue in the future.

## THE MIDDLE ROAD

Lao Tzu suggests that leaders take a middle road, embracing both sides of a debate or issue. In chapter 28 of the *Tao Te Ching*, he writes:

> Know the masculine, hold to the feminine . . .
> Know the white, hold to the black . . .
> Know the honor, hold to the humility. (Lin 2006, 57)

Good leaders know the value of each end of a continuum. While the best way to be might be humble, the principal should also understand the value of honor. In each of the lines above, Lao Tzu recommends going with the gentler, less aggressive way to proceed. At the same time, he knows that a good leader has to know when to be aggressive or highly visible in his dealings as well.

By being somewhere in the middle, the principal can wait to commit herself. If she commits too early, there may be no turning back without humiliation. Keeping all options open allows the principal to gather as much information as possible before acting.

Lao Tzu continues this concept:

> Return to the state of plain wood
> Plain wood splits, then becomes tools
> The sages utilize them
> And then become leaders. (Lin 2006, 57)

Here again, the admonition is to hold back as long as possible. A block of wood has endless potential, which is its power. Once the wood is carved into a tool, the potential is gone. Consequently it behooves the leader to wait, not to be hasty in committing.

Imagine that there is a budget cut coming. The principal starts preparing the staff for the worst. He has determined how many positions the cut will eliminate, it not which ones specifically. The staff panics, and their productivity and effectiveness falter as a result of this ominous atmosphere. Then, when the time comes, the board finds several areas, such as maintenance, to cut without touching staff.

The principal could have maintained a better climate had he not immediately translated the coming board action in the most negative way possible. He gets everyone worked up for nothing.

He would have spent his time more wisely building an argument for keeping all staff positions and where there might be alternative cuts, if he eventually needed it. In the meantime, he could have quietly reassured any teachers who expressed fear of a cut by telling them that no decision had yet been made.

Chapter 29 continues this theme of moderation, explaining that the leader should avoid absolutes. Any excess is a problem (Lin 2006, 59).

Lao Tzu bluntly states to simply avoid too much of anything. Keep to a balanced approach. Do not embrace anything to excess.

Again, the principal may force herself into a corner by arguing strongly for one position early in the process rather than holding off. Excess can refer to either side of an argument or condition. Finally, the principal should eschew arrogance (Lin, 59) She should not assume that she is right and everyone else wrong. She should not act without regard for others' feelings or thoughts. This is a sure route to alienation.

## HUMILITY

Throughout Taoism, the idea of humility is paramount.

> The Master stays behind;
> that is why she is ahead.
> She is detached from all things;
> that is why she is one with them.
> Because she has let go of herself,
> She is perfectly fulfilled. (Mitchell 1988, 7)

Despite their putting themselves behind, the wise leaders "float" to the top, having gained everyone's respect. They work for others, not themselves. In the process, their own goals get taken care of. If you want improved nutrition in the cafeteria, is it not better to ask those who prepare the food what to do rather than telling them what new recipes to prepare? People naturally do not like being pushed around. But a humble leader is inclined to win over the staff.

The leader avoids attachment, valuing one thing over another. She remains personally unconnected with the situation. There is no ego, no bias. Her deliberations are pure. In this way, she is actually one with everything, offending nothing.

Sun Tzu reinforces these ideas:

> Thus one advances without seeking glory, retreats without avoiding blame, only protecting people to the benefit of the government as well, thus rendering valuable service to the nation. (Cleary 1988, 137)

The respected leader is not out for glory, but interested in taking the right action for others' sake. He is willing to take the blame for failure rather than passing it on to someone else. If he is successful, he is quiet about it (Lin 2006, 19).

If a principal allows herself to take too much note of others' judgment of her, she will be unable to handle a situation with objectivity and clear thinking. Doing the right thing may not be the popular position, and a principal has to accept this. Otherwise she is playing to the audience, to approval, rather than to the truth. She is afraid of being devalued in the eyes of others.

> Favor and disgrace make one fearful
> The greatest misfortune is the self
> What does "favor and disgrace make one fearful" mean?
> Favor is high; disgrace is low
> Having it makes one fearful
> Losing it makes one fearful
> This is "favor and disgrace make one fearful." (Lin 2006, 27)

If the leader is in a position of favor, he fears losing it. If he is in a position of disgrace, he is fearful of the opinion of others about him. By caring for the ego, or self, the principal can lose sight of the bigger picture. The goals are not about the leader. They are about the staff, students, parents, and institution.

Sometimes a principal will recommend someone for a job because the person and she are friends. The principal wants to be admired by the other. Perhaps one paraprofessional must be cut in order to balance the budget. The popular response would be to fight for the position. The responsible action would be to determine which person to let go. Once the ego and the need to be in favor take over, the leader can easily lose her objective wisdom.

The best leaders are so quiet about their work, and so self-effacing, that when a task is accomplished, their staffs believe that they are personally responsible for the success of the situation (Lin, 35). Humility prevails, and the leader avoids fame and praise, easily giving them away.

The Tao itself stands as an exemplar of humility. All things depend on it. It does what needs to be done without notice (Lin, 69).

Nurturing is more important then gaining praise or credit. The wise leader takes care of the staff without them believing that they owe him something. Lao Tzu admonishes his readers, "He doesn't glitter like a jewel" (Mitchell, 39).

The Mitchell translation sums up this section nicely in chapter 66:

> All streams flow to the sea
> because it is lower than they are.
> Humility gives it its power. (Mitchell 1988, 66)

## CASE STUDY 1

*You are the principal of a K–6 school in a suburban area. Your school needs a new reading program. The staff is about equally divided between phonics and whole language approaches. There are excellent teachers on both sides of the arguments. A number of teachers from each position have asked to speak with you privately to lobby for their position.*

*The board is also divided between the two approaches. They have done their research and cannot decide which approach would have the best results for their students. At this point, parents are getting involved as well. A group of influential parents has formed to study the issue. There are scheduled to present their findings in two weeks.*

*In the meantime, a teacher committee has been established, also to study the efficacy of the two approaches.*

*You are carefully watching all of this unfold. Your own experience tells you to go with phonics, but you have not said anything directly yet. You know that the board will eventually ask for your professional opinion. At this point you are not sure what position to take. You have been reading journal articles about reading teaching methods to try to become well acquainted with the topic.*

*To complicate matters, you have a brother-in-law who sells whole language materials for a large publishing house. A board member also has a relation who sells reading materials, but this time phonics. You do not want to offend anyone, but the chances are that you will. You want to satisfy the board, your staff, and the parents group without alienating anyone.*

*The newspaper has gotten wind of the situation, and they have begun to run articles describing each of the two reading methodologies, interviewing experts and reviewing materials. They have been pressing you for some kind of answer or at least a preference.*

*The budget will be completed in two months, so the decision will have to be made by then in order to set aside enough money to fund whichever program you choose. What are you going to do?*

1. Which ideas from the chapter can you apply to this situation?
2. Is there a way to avoid alienating anybody in the decision-making process?
3. Where should you go for advice?
4. What are you going to tell the teachers who are coming to talk with you about the decision?
5. How will personal matters play into your decision?
6. How can you do the right thing without appearing to favor one group over another?
7. How will you deal with those who don't get their way?
8. How will you approach the board?

## CASE STUDY 2

*During the summer, your board adopted a student dress policy. Boys are to wear collared shirts, khaki pants, and nonathletic shoes. Girls are to wear a blouse and skirt or pants or a dress, and again there are no athletic shoes. Jeans are not allowed.*

*School opens with the usual flurry of activity. Naturally, students are not pleased with the new policy. As anticipated, there is a break-in period when students test the new code, violating it to see what happens. There are protests, from both parents and students. Teachers are annoyed that they have to police one more aspect of student behavior.*

*Despite all this, and with consistency of implementation, everyone settles down and accepts the dress code as something here to stay. Everything is running smoothly.*

*Two months into the year, Robert Jakes moves into the district and enrolls in your school. He is out of compliance with the dress code his first few days at school. You assume that this is simply a period during which Robert is adjusting to his new situation. However, by the second week you expect him to understand the code.*

*On the first day of his second week, Robert is still wearing athletic shoes. Several teachers and students are complaining that he has had enough time to understand what he needs to do. They think he should be suspended for each day he is out of compliance, the penalty specified in the policy.*

*In your career as an administrator, you have become used to having students do what you tell them to. You do not have discussions; you gently but firmly lay down the law. So you are quite surprised at what Robert has to tell you when he comes to your office.*

*Robert does not have any regular shoes. The athletic foot wear he is wearing, in fact, are hand-me-downs from his older brother. He has spoken with his parents about the problem, but they are not willing to spend the money on new shoes when the ones he is wearing are perfectly adequate in their eyes. Robert's dad has recently lost his job, so money is tight.*

*What are you going to do? If you do not apply the policy as written, certainly teachers, students, parents, and board members will have something to say. Can you appear to be weak on this issue? What will you say on the phone to Robert's parents? What will you say to other students and their parents when they have already had to pay the penalty for violating the dress code? Can you successfully deal with Robert, save face, and maintain the policy? You have never had a problem like this before.*

1. Whicht aspects of the chapter can you apply to this scenario?
2. Should the policy be changed, and if so, how?
3. What would suspending Robert accomplish?
4. To whom will you appeal for assistance in this matter?
5. Do you think finding other students who have had Robert's problem and asking them what they did could help?
6. Is Robert a special case deserving special consideration?
7. How will you deal with teachers who are always looking for weakness in you, especially around discipline issues?
8. In what ways has your world changed? How will you adapt to these changes?

# Conclusion

East or West? This is not such an easy question. The point, however, is that there is a choice at all. A leader does not have to have one approach that fits every situation. There are alternatives to win-lose, control styles.

Being slow and contemplative is not being weak. Being humble does not indicate a lack of leadership. Respecting the enemy does not mean giving in. No two situations are the same, and the successful leader selects his tools and actions to fit the circumstances.

There are many examples, scenarios, and problems in this book. The author has applied a Taoist approach to them. Some seem forced, but others flow more naturally. Surely, many readers could apply alternative approaches to these situations with great success.

The book does not argue for one approach being superior to the other. It simply illustrates a particular approach. It does argue that some characteristics of leadership which are anathema to a Western style might prove quite useful, despite their unfamiliarity or unpopularity.

There are many individuals who already use some of the Eastern approaches in their leadership. Such strategies are, in fact, not exclusive to Eastern thinking. Certainly there are traditions of humility, tolerance for ambiguity, and caution before action in our own society. Taoism just seems to be a well-developed set of beliefs incorporating all of these features.

The win-lose game puts unnecessary pressure on everyone. The leader is desperate to win. Losing is intolerable. Others see this same thing from the other side. They will not be beaten by an unfair leader or situation. They will come out victorious in the end.

The metaphor with the military and battle used by Sun Tzu is apt in this case. Of course if we speak of winners and losers, the next step is to speak of conflict, friends and enemies, and battle. Is there really any place for this in educational leadership?

Actual fighting, as Sun Tzu explains, is detrimental to all parties. A leader should avoid it whenever possible. The best way to win a battle is by not fighting in the first place. Either be so well-fortified that you are unassailable, or avoid battle through some other planning and strategy.

Fighting is costly for the leader. Even if he wins, at what price has he done so? Has the school climate changed for the worse? Are his "enemies" now a solidified group? Has he lost friends? Is it a Pyrrhic victory at best? Have others been made to feel like losers? Avoiding the fight may have been a better course of action.

Perhaps there are circumstances when conflict and battle are unavoidable. There are times when a principal must stem the progress of irrational forces, of individuals with personal agendas, of those who cannot see the bigger picture beyond themselves.

Taking the extra time to reflect can be difficult in this fast-paced and sometimes chaotic world in which we live and work. Each moment can be precious, not to be wasted. However, if a leader can accept that time spent on reflection is part of the time spent on resolving an issue, then spending that time becomes not extra but part of the problem-solving process.

Being an educational leader is not a competition. It is a position from which to steer the school in a productive and positive direction. Not only then does the principal have to be humble, but also she has to act from a position of virtue. She has to do what is morally and ethically right. In the end, everyone in the institution should feel fairly heard, should feel a part of the solution, and should feel a part of the whole. Competitive strife cannot accomplish this.

While competition applied productively can inspire individuals or groups to do their best, applied incorrectly it can destroy a school climate. An autocratic leader breeds anxiety among the staff. People can be reluctant to speak their minds for fear of reprisals. The full examination of an issue is not possible. People need support, not suppression.

Winning for the sake of winning is an egotistical endeavor which ignores the best solution for the sake of one's own position. This is not the model we want to present to our students. If we want them to become thoughtful debaters and problem solvers, then we have to show them what this looks like through our own behaviors. The leader must hold the moral, ethical, and logical line for the institution.

Another peculiar perception we hold about leadership is what we misconstrue as steadfastness. If a principal changes her mind, we call that being inconsistent or wishy-washy. Why would you stick with a plan which is not working? What happens when circumstances change or the leader gets new information which changes the reality of the situation?

If a doctor were treating a patient, and that treatment did not work, would you not want him to try something else? In the book, the author developed the example of the student who could not afford the shoes necessary for being in compliance with the dress code. Should that student be suspended for the infraction, since that is the rule? Must we maintain our stance or point of view regardless of what is happening?

Sun Tzu certainly understand this issue. He would call an inflexible leader a fool. He knew that being prepared for all circumstances was crucial to success. He recognized the world as fluid, changing all the tine. He realized that the good leader would flow with events, not simply blindly apply one idea to a situation.

Leadership positions can easily become about the leader and not about the institution. After all, these positions always entail having power and authority. They feed the ego of the incumbent. Needing to be right, needing to get one's own way, is a natural outcome in these cases.

The leader must always remember to put others first, before himself. The institution is more important than the principal's career. A productive, trusting staff is more important than winning an argument or getting one's way. This is particularly difficult to do when the tendency is for everyone to be looking at the leader for action and a solution to the current problem. The principal has to be simultaneously powerful and humble.

Remember that losing the battle can be winning the war. If the vast majority opposes the leader on an issue of lesser import, such as an element of the dress code, giving in may be in order. By so doing, the principal loses little if anything, and at the same time projects an image of support and acceptance of others and their ideas. Giving away the victory and taking the loss can be a powerful strategy for leadership.

Positions of leadership are often lonely. There is not the same peer group enjoyed by teachers or other staff. In order to ameliorate the isolation of her position, a principal would be wise to forge positive relationships with others rather than destroying them through the use of autocratic, egocentric techniques.

Principals need to stand ready to learn from others and follow the directions they set. In other words, the leader should take his cue from "the people." This is the ultimate expression of humility, respecting what everyone has to offer. No one has exclusive rights to the best or correct answer to a problem.

Another art of leadership is being able to read a situation. The principal cannot allow her own position and opinion to blind her to what is going on. How many times have you thought you understood what was happening when you discovered that people's actions and motivations were not at all what you thought them to be?

The successful leader takes into account all of the forces and energy flows of what is happening. There is no sense in rowing against the tide unless the principal fears being ethically compromised by opposing points of view. Sometimes you just have to take a stand.

Reading a situation is the reason to be slow to act. A leader needs to understand the forces he is dealing with before committing to a course of action. What do people really want? Where is the situation heading generally? Can you use the forces at hand to solve the problem, rather than trying to control events and change the course of the inevitable.

Lao Tzu uses the image of the block of wood to illustrate the need for deliberate action. A block of wood has the potential to be many things. However, once it is carved into a specific tool, all that potential is gone. In the same way, the wise leader waits before committing to a specific course of action, holding on to maximum potential paths until the best one becomes clear.

Take another look at the problematic dress code. You may have proposed a perfectly reasonable code, but you find teachers, students, and parents in opposition. Are they opposed because they disagree with aspects of your proposal, or is it that they feel that they have not been included in the decision-making process?

Clearly, you will act differently depending on which way you read the situation. If people do not like what you have put forth, then the answer may be to have more conversation explaining what you are doing and the justification for it. If people are feeling left out of the process, then you must devise methods for their voices to be seriously heard. In either case, you work with the flow of energy, not against it, not trying to control it.

Taoism offers a manner of observing and working with the world which is much different from the stereotypical Western approach. Putting winners and losers aside, embracing humility, and being contemplative can lead to more effective leadership and a climate of community. The leader holds on to the moral high ground, modeling virtue and fairness for the entire institution.

Educational leaders stand to learn much and gain effectiveness by studying Taoism as part of the preservice or inservice training. They can start by engaging the case studies in this book to practice different ways to solve problems.

# References

Bright-Fey, John, Trans. (2006) *Tao, the complete teachings from the oral tradition of lao-tzu*. Birmingham, AL: Crane Hill Publishers.
Cleary, T., Trans. (1988). *The art of war* (Sun Tzu). Boston: Shambhala Publications, Inc.
Dale, A. D., Trans. (2002) *Tao te ching* (Lao Tzu). New York: Barnes and Noble Publishing.
Denma Translation Group. (2001) *The art of war* (Sun Tzu). Boston: Shambhala Publications.
Lin, Derek, Trans. (2006). *Tao te ching* (Lao Tzu). Woodstock, VT: SkyLight Paths Publishing.
Mitchell, Stephan, Trans. (1988). *Tao te ching* (Lao Tzu). New York: Harper & Row.
Sorajjakool, Siroj. (2001). *Wu wei, negativity and depression*. Binghamton, NY: The Haworth Pastoral Press.

# About the Author

**Daniel Heller** served as a teacher and administrator for more than thirty years. Now retired, he has written numerous articles and five books about educational topics. He takes as major themes kindness, equity, and supervision. Heller holds master's degrees in English and education, and an honorary doctorate from St. Joseph's College in Rutland, Vermont. He lives in Brattleboro, Vermont, with his wife of thirty-six years and his Labrador Retriever.

www.ingramcontent.com/pod-product-compliance
Lightning Source LLC
Chambersburg PA
CBHW020753230426

**43665CB00009B/579**